THE *CRAZY* MOTHER'S

GUIDE TO

RAISING EXCEPTIONAL

CHILDREN

THE *CRAZY* MOTHER'S GUIDE TO RAISING EXCEPTIONAL CHILDREN

THE *CRAZY* MOTHER'S GUIDE TO RAISING EXCEPTIONAL CHILDREN

An Aussie Mum's First-Hand Experience With Parenting Children Who Have Autism Spectrum Disorder and Dissociative Identity Disorder.

By Sonia D. Hebdon

Edited by A.E. Marshall

Copyright © 2024, Sonia D. Hebdon "All rights reserved."

No part of this publication may be reproduced, distributed, or transmitted in any form or by any manner, including photocopying, recording, or other electronic or mechanical methods, without the prior written permission of the publisher, except in the case of brief quotations embodied in reviews and certain other non-commercial uses permitted by copyright law.

Paperback ISBN: 978-1-7638147-0-7

eBook ISBN: 978-1-7638147-1-4

"First Edition: December 2024" AUSTRALIA

Copyright © Cover Design J.F.E. Marshall

Illustrations created with Recraft a-i art.

Edited by A.E. Marshall / Publisher: J.F.E. Marshall

Description: The Crazy Mother's Guide To Raising Exceptional Children

An Aussie Mum's First-Hand Experience With Parenting Children Who Have Autism Spectrum Disorder and Dissociative Identity Disorder

Sonia D. Hebdon

Audience: Parents of children/teens with ASD/ DID. Christian parenting strategies for kids with mental health issues. 230 pages, black & white photos & illustrations.

Author's note

Most of the names in this book have been changed to protect individuals' privacy. Some participants gave permission for their real names to be used, and my daughter and son gave permission for incidents involving them to be included in this book.

Trigger Warning!

This book discusses distressing issues regarding self-harm and suicidal ideation. Please be aware that the author talks about tough topics in order to share her own practical strategies for dealing with these situations. Whether to adopt some of the parenting techniques mentioned in this book is purely at the reader's discretion.

Legal Disclaimer

The information presented in this book is the author's (Sonia D. Hebdon) opinion only and does not constitute any health or medical advice. The content of this book is for informational purposes only and is not intended to diagnose, treat, cure, or prevent any condition or disease. If you or your loved one is in a life-threatening or emergency medical situation, seek medical assistance immediately. Sonia D. Hebdon and J.F.E. Marshall, the publisher, are not legally responsible for failing the advice in this disclaimer! Please seek advice from your healthcare provider for your personal health concerns before following the advice in this book.

DEDICATION

This book is dedicated to my amazing husband Adam, my 'partner in crime' on this hair-raising journey, who has always picked me up when I felt I couldn't take any more parenting nightmares. I also dedicate this book to my 'Jedi Master' – my spiritual advisor Pastor Chris J., who has discipled me throughout my Christian growth, which is grounded in the two greatest commandments, as taught by Jesus:

> *"Love the Lord your God with all your heart and with all your soul and with all your mind"* and *"Love your neighbour as yourself."* – Matthew 22:37 & 39

To Ceils, my gorgeous friend, hero, and oracle: You inspire me, and I am so proud to have you in my life. A big hug to the coolest vegetarian I know, Snaz, who was my rock during my husband's 'health crisis' and my Cure concert partner. To my best friend Balfour, thank you for encouraging me to write and always supporting me when I needed you.

Most importantly, to my two incredible children and my alter kids, Genevieve and Edmund, thank you for teaching me patience and kindness by pushing me to cling to my faith and praying that God will work it all out for the better, no matter how bleak the situation is. Lastly, a huge thanks to my father who, as an amputee, taught me the importance of maintaining a sense of humour to help cope with stressful situations and to treat all people with disabilities fairly, kindly, and respectfully.

My 'hero dad' proudly showing off a one-kilo birthday celebration steak, which he devoured like a lion consuming its prey.

ACKNOWLEDGEMENTS

Thanks to Nick and Billie-Jo, our Disability Support Coordinators, who have helped so much with our kids, thanks to their passion for improving disabled people's lives. I also want to thank our distance education teachers who have provided valuable assistance and guidance for our children over the past seven years: Brenda, Brent, Jonathan, Liz, Rita, Sarah, and amazing Taryn for their enthusiastic approach to education.

A special shout-out to our Disability Support Workers, particularly Brittany, Caitlin, Lisa, Mitch, Poppy, Rhys, Russell, Tatiana and the many helpers working with our children. They come to our home with warm smiles and enthusiastically assist our children. Disability Support Workers are the front-line soldiers in our battles who take the shots and keep coming back for more.

Please check out the social media links at the back of the book for further information on joining the *Crazy* Mothers' Support Group and sharing your fabulous, true parenting stories.

TABLE OF CONTENTS

Introduction	p. 1
Chapter 1: It Started With A Kiss	p. 7
Chapter 2: Your Child Is A Superhero	p. 17
Chapter 3: Why Fit In When You Were Meant To Stand Out	p. 30
Chapter 4: Keep The Faith	p. 40
Chapter 5: Def Con One	p. 58
Chapter 6: Filter, Filter, Filter	p. 64
Chapter 7: I'm Off To Join The Circus	p. 73
Chapter 8: Time To Get Crazy: Outside Of The Box Parenting Tips	p. 84
Chapter 9: Expect The Unexpected	p. 91
Chapter 10: Time To Forgive Yourself And Others	p. 115
Chapter 11: Saying Sorry	p. 122

TABLE OF CONTENTS

Chapter 12: Getting Organised — p.127

Chapter 13: Selecting The Right Pieces For Your Puzzle — p.137

Chapter 14: Rescue Therapy — p.143

Chapter 15: New Experiences — p.151

Chapter 16: Forming Connections — p.157

Chapter 17: Growing Up — p.170

Chapter 18: The Unknown — p.176

Chapter 19: What I Have Learned On This Incredible Journey — p.182

Chapter 20: Crazy Mother's Guide To Raising Exceptional Children – The 12 Principles — p.197

Chapter 21: What Does Your Future Hold? — p.204

INTRODUCTION

This is a parenting book like no other. As a Christian mother of two special needs children, I would often discuss with friends how crazy my life is, parenting these unique individuals. I have a charismatic, 12-year-old, High-functioning ASD (Autism Spectrum Disorder) boy and a beautiful, 19-year-old ASD girl who also has Dissociative Identity Disorder (DID), formerly known as Multiple Personality Disorder. She was diagnosed with DID in her mid-teens, which is unusually young as it isn't until their twenties that DID people typically begin noticing the memory blanks that occur in their lives when their 'alters' or different personalities emerge.

My daughter's mind has numerous 'parts' of differing ages. On one occasion, my alter-daughter Cleo – 29 years of age – approached me to ask for "a cigarette and some booze." This first occurred when my daughter was 16 and too young to drink or smoke in Australia legally. My solution was to pop an umbrella straw into a glass of lemonade, and handing it to her, I said, "Here's your mocktail. You're too young to drink." Cleo grabbed her alcohol-free drink in disgust. She muttered, "I get better service at McDonald's." Cleo is one of my daughter's many parts in the system, taking more of an internal role as my daughter enters adulthood. However, the two parts that front the most often – Edmund and Genevieve – still appear now and then, typically when Ruby experiences a trigger. These two colourful identities feature heavily in my family's personal story.

Do you remember the well-meaning family and friends who idealised motherhood during your pregnancy? Coupled with glossy magazine depictions of mothers who looked like they had just stepped out of a beauty salon instead of a birthing room, pregnancy is often portrayed as pure joy! However, my own experience was quite the opposite.

The magazines made no mention of the extreme nausea and violent vomiting I endured during morning sickness. I was also unprepared for the life-threatening medical issue called pre-eclampsia – high blood pressure that can lead to seizures – and the consequent emergency C-section when I went into labour. Compounding this was my baby's brow presentation, which meant she couldn't pass through the birth canal without severely damaging her facial features and threatening my life due to haemorrhaging. Additionally, a clumsily performed anaesthetic spinal tap left me with permanent numbness in the heel of my left foot, accompanied by ongoing severe, localised back pain around the injection site in my lower back.

My second pregnancy was marked by even worse nausea than the first; so severe was the retching that I tore my abdominal muscles, and the persistent sickness was debilitating and depressing. That pregnancy also concluded with a C-section, as is advised for births following an initial C-section being performed on a mother. Thankfully, all that suffering was rewarded with two big, beautiful, healthy babies born seven years apart.

Yet, unbeknown to me in the early stages of their lives, my children were born with High-functioning Autism (formerly known as Aspergers Syndrome). Our daughter would eventually develop Dissociative Identity Disorder and experience other mental health conditions as well.

"Well, they didn't mention my children's health issues in those parenting magazines", I would say with a hurt, mocking smile as I reflected worryingly on my children's diagnoses with my closest friends. Soon enough, I also discovered that precious little was written to inform, advise or encourage parents in their daily dealings with the crazy, unusual parenting dilemmas that autistic children present. There was almost nothing at all written for parents of children with Dissociative Identity Disorder.

So, I offer my unique stories, reflections, and insights from raising my special kids to encourage and assist other parents in similar circumstances. Having kept a journal over the years, which is loaded with many humorous incidents associated with my children's disorders, I knew that eventually – sometime in the near-distant future – I would compile our family's story. And now, here it is …

This book is for all the parents who have been emotionally drained by their special needs kids and found themselves dreaming of packing a suitcase and running off with the circus. In my social media accounts, I often post cartoon pictures of clowns in cars, imagining I'm one of them, escaping to some unknown, happy and carefree place. This would become my 'bat signal' to close friends, alerting them that I had a bad day and needed to talk with someone who understood the craziness of my life. They often reminded me that wanting to escape the insanity is quite normal and feeling this way is entirely okay. However, sharing my stories with other mums of special needs children taught me that every parenting situation is unique and often requires unusual parenting techniques.

Parents of ASD kids are often unfairly judged when their children have meltdowns in public places, which happens due to their hyper-sensory issues. The disapproving and judgemental glares from parents of neurotypical (normal or regular) kids can leave us doubting our parenting abilities and can damage our self-confidence. All parents of special needs children have been embarrassed by public criticism, and I salute all these fantastic parents who go through life dealing with insane situations and yet are judged by family members and friends, as well as strangers who don't understand what parenting these kids entails.

I address mental health issues such as suicidal depression and self-harm extensively in this book from my personal, first-hand experiences with our beautiful teenage daughter. Ruby has often had to fight just to get out of bed in the morning, depressed from the childhood trauma that sparked her DID, exacerbated by her High-functioning Autism. It's a tough life.

I have discovered the power of support networks for parents of special needs children. We can form strong connections by sharing our experiences with others facing similar challenges. To that end, please join our positive support network through the social media links provided at the end of this book for affirming, positive, caring friendships with like-minded parents. I have often heard the African Proverb, "It takes a village to raise a child." I wholeheartedly believe that parents of special needs children can unite and create a fantastic world and future for their children.

CHAPTER 1
IT STARTED WITH A KISS

The bond between a mother and child is quite extraordinary. I still remember when I held my babies for the first time: the softness of their skin, the touch of their tiny hands on my face. These are intimate, bonding moments that all mums remember fondly. I was an older mother and gave birth to my daughter in my early 30s and my son in my late 30s. Both were C-section deliveries due to medical complications during my pregnancies, and my two children are 'rainbow babies' – I miscarried two babies years before.

The first kiss on their foreheads, the exhausted, sheer relief of finally having them in my arms! I looked into my babies' innocent, inquiring eyes and saw limitless possibilities for their future. What marvels will these new souls perform? To what heights could they climb? Was I looking at a future doctor? A lawyer? My imagination was fired by the new hope and joy embodied in their fresh lives. I imagined a family home with a white picket fence and my children playing with a dog in the yard completed my idyllic vision.

As a new mother, I wasn't aware that health complications could bring about positive changes in my life, but when my children were first diagnosed, there was fear, heartbreak and concern over what my kids' future might hold. I read parenting books offering advice on raising children, but ten years ago, I was utterly oblivious to Autism Spectrum Disorder or Dissociative Identity Disorder and was starting from a position of complete ignorance in these matters. Before their diagnoses (both were diagnosed around the same time), all I knew was that I finally had my perfect children and would do everything possible to be a great mum. I never thought I would be pulling 20 Matchbox cars out of our toilet, a gift to me that my two-year-old son had deposited there. Or that I would find myself cleaning four litres of cooking oil, a full two-kilo bag's worth of plain flour and three bottles of food dye out of my rented home's lounge room carpet. And another 'gift' – a big poo – would be deposited in the bathtub within an hour of my taking care of the carpet mess!

Yes, I am talking about our son 'Dennis The Menace.' He had the most fantastic corkscrew curls and would readily throw his emptied baby bottles across the room like a drunken sailor. The first indication that he was different was when he developed an early childhood obsession with manholes ('maintenance holes' in America). When he was two, we lived beside a park that kangaroos often visited. I would excitedly point them out to him from the front porch, "Look sweetheart, a kangaroo." Our son would look up at me and point elsewhere, saying, "Look mummy, a manhole." I would attempt to correct him, "No honey, a kangaroo!" But he would brush me off and, with some agitation in his little voice, repeat, "Look, mummy, a manhole!" So when we went driving anywhere, we played a game we invented called "count the manholes" on the side of the road.

I vividly recall the time I was watching him playing nicely on the lounge room floor with his recently deceased grandpa's mobile (cell) phone. My husband and I agreed to take the SIM card out, thinking it would make an excellent toy for our son. The little boy was yabbering away playfully into the phone whilst seated on the floor when I received a phone call on our landline from Emergency Services. He was three at the time, and no one had taught him to dial Triple-Zero (911 in America) and how it is used in emergencies. "Hello, do you have a son talking on the mobile phone of a deceased elderly man?" I said, "Yes, but he's pretending to talk to his grandma." Confused, I grabbed the mobile phone, and when I heard the emergency operator's voice on the other end, I suddenly became very aware of what was happening.

If this were a movie, there would be a triple-zoom reflex close-up on my horrified face as I realised what my son had done. What I thought was an imaginary discussion with grandma proved to be an actual, twenty-minute conversation with an Emergency Services operator, the boy telling her all about how big his poopies were and how kangaroos liked manholes. My husband and I weren't aware that mobile phones can still call Emergency Services without a SIM card. Imagine my surprise when a local police officer arrived to ensure everything was okay.

There are days when I feel tremendously motivated as a parent to help my children achieve something special for the day. But then there are days when I want to hide when they call my name. Parenting special needs children is exhausting and stressful but also challenging and rewarding. Honestly, all parents of children with disabilities deserve an award because only a Hollywood comedy writer could think of the kind of bizarre events that occur daily in our lives.

Our 19-year-old daughter is a perfect example of a fantastic teenager living a bizarre and unusual life. She has ASD and Dissociative Identity Disorder. DID is caused by childhood trauma, and my daughter's brain has formed several distinct personalities who are gate-keepers and holders of knowledge about specific experiences hidden behind an 'amnesia wall' until the time came for her alters and their information to be revealed and explain the cause of her anxiety and depression. When her medical professionals explained this concept to me, I had a mental image of the Berlin Wall falling. This massive memory wall, compartmentalising my daughter's experiences, had turned to rubble, and the formerly hidden alters entered the real world to see the sun and the moon for the first time.

Ruby has numerous different personalities, and in hindsight, there were signs she had this disorder for years. When she was younger, she would talk in distinctive voices and want to be called by different names. Her personality and facial expressions would change like she was a different child. And then she couldn't recall conversations we'd had. Our daughter is the inspiration for this book. Every day, I face the challenge of mothering not only my daughter but also her alters.

Ranging widely in age and gender, her alters have different accents, handwriting, belief systems and personalities. For example, Cleo – our daughter's 28-year-old alter with a British accent – is wilful and quite a handful. Every time Cleo emerged, we'd do the same dance, arguing over her demands for booze and cigarettes. This happened so frequently for a while that I felt stuck in Groundhog Day, which was exhausting. I don't know how often I told her, "It isn't going to happen. You are in my daughter's 16-year-old body." Though we performed this dance repeatedly like a broken record, I admire her determination to keep trying to get her way.

Parents of special needs children are honoured for their self-sacrificial dedication in raising their often-times difficult children under challenging circumstances. I reflect on many sleepless nights, tears and triumphs, criticisms and approvals – most often from my own extended family – and now I want to share my personal and unusual parenting experiences in the hope of encouraging other mothers who are dealing with similar circumstances and feel isolated due to their children's disabilities.

My husband and I have faced the most bizarre parenting dilemmas together. It is relevant to know that alters, like animals or mythical creatures, can be non-human. Alters can also disappear quickly and become absorbed by other alters or no longer exist. This happens when your child has achieved a milestone or made a realisation that is very important to the traumatic circumstances under which the alters were first created. What is interesting is that during times of crisis, the child can also gain new alters as their brain has adapted to creating new personalities as a strategy for dealing with distressing situations.

Laughter is essential for parenting special needs children, as we are exposed daily to strange and unusual events and experiences. Cracking a joke and laughing to blow off steam can diffuse mounting tension from a situation and reduce it to manageable proportions, allowing for concrete solutions to problems. You feel like a teapot on a stove; when the steam builds up, you need to release the pressure; otherwise, you'll end up in a corner, weaving baskets and banging your head against a padded wall.

So, laughter is the best medicine for you as a parent. Your child needs to know that you are not making fun of them or putting them down. You are laughing at the strange situation they have put you in, problems that are never discussed in parenting books. This is the motivation for the preparation of this memoir, together with lessons learned from my personal experiences. Please understand that the title of this book is not making fun of my children. It is about having a light-hearted sense of humour when dealing with strange and wonderful parenting situations we have encountered as parents of children with Autism and Dissociative Identity Disorder.

We desperately love our children and want them to have a relatively normative life, but we know they constantly face many challenges. There will be days when we make brilliant progress and other days when we want to go into the bathroom and scream our heads off, yelling profanities like kettles blow off steam. This is normal and nothing to feel guilty about: losing your cool or feeling completely lost – like drowning in a sea of turbulent waves – is to be expected. You need to accept that you are a fallible human, which God knows all too well. Learning to forgive yourself as God forgives you is essential to getting out of bed in the morning and facing a new day with enthusiasm and strength. Be encouraged by the stories I will share with you, which actually happened and are not fabricated. Please know that you are not alone and that the world, although a properly scary place, is also filled with limitless possibilities for making positive changes in your child's life. So, join the crazy mothers' revolution and see the glass half full and not half empty!

Please reach out to other parents of special needs children and establish support networks of your own. In these networks, you can share your problems and contribute to helping other parents with disabled children have productive and rewarding lives. Their perspectives have changed my outlook on dealing with the crazy experiences I face with our two amazing and talented kids. Never give up hope! Tomorrow is a new day filled with endless possibilities for your children to achieve great things.

CHAPTER 2
YOUR CHILD IS A SUPERHERO

When I was a little girl in kindergarten, I adored Wonder Woman. I was four when the boys at my kindy often dressed in superhero costumes, racing madly around the playground. My mother knew I felt left out, so she made me a Wonder Woman costume. This was in the late 1970s when store-bought costumes were uncommon and expensive. So my mother spent hours at her sewing machine, madly creating her version of the iconic outfit. I stood in front of the mirror admiring my sudden transformation from ordinary child to superhero or in my case, supervillain. I only had the costume for two weeks when my mother was called to my kindergarten to discuss my misbehaviour.

I have told my kids this story hundreds of times: I wanted to be Wonder Woman because the little superhero boys who were supposed to be doing good and fighting crime were bullying the other kids in the playground whenever the childcare workers had their backs turned. I took matters into my own hands and kicked sand in their faces, hit one mean boy in the shoulder with his prized toy dump truck and hid all the smaller toy trucks the superhero gang was playing with around the play area. I remember smiling mischievously as all the bully boys were reduced to tears, but Wonder Woman taught them a lesson!

Many parents don't realise their special needs children are superheroes. Most of our beloved comic superheroes have incredible powers but also life-threatening weaknesses. For example, Superman looks great in tights and can fly; he has X-ray vision, phenomenal strength and speed, is good-looking and has an incredible physique. However, his major weakness is the dreaded Kryptonite. Once exposed to this green crystal, he becomes incapacitated and can die from the crippling effects.

Marvel Comics is offering some positivity for neurologically atypical kids with their latest superhero Moon Knight, who has DID. But most heroes' double-life natures have DID-like presentations. The Incredible Hulk displays DID and ASD traits, as Bruce Banner and his alter-ego are reminiscent of Robert Louis Stevenson's Dr. Jekyll and Mr. Hyde's split personalities.

For example, the Hulk's meltdowns represent a child with ASD. I have often used this character to explain ASD symptoms to my child. Dr Bruce Banner is a good-looking and mild-mannered scientist, but due to an experiment in his lab that went wrong, he becomes The Incredible Hulk when subjected to extreme stress. Does this sound similar to an ASD child's meltdown?

When Bruce loses control, he turns green, becomes enraged, and destroys everything standing in his way. I can see the similarity with my daughter's meltdowns when she was younger. One minute, she's rational and happy; the next, she's out of control and in a wild rage, unable to offer more than one-word answers until the meltdown passes, almost always triggered by something seemingly inconsequential. This metamorphosis into a giant green monster with no manners or restraint represents DID. Bruce Banner's alter ego, The Hulk, emerges as a mean, green fighting machine, ready to destroy the wicked oppressors who have antagonised him into these fits of uncontrollable rage.

Thanks to his wrist-mounted web spinner, Spiderman can swing across town at high speed, suspended above the crowds and traffic. However, he is vulnerable to Ethyl Chloride and water, which weakens his reflexes and speed. Bruce Wayne created Batman to avenge the brutal murder of his parents. He trained himself to become a specialist in many areas, but his greatest weakness is overconfidence. He alienates his allies by believing he can handle every situation by himself.

How does the superhero metaphor relate to your children? All special needs kids are gifted in at least one particular competency, such as music, art, technology or sport. Our daughter was reading 200-page books in her first school year. The same year, she was placed in the school's gifted art program. In year three, she was awarded a trophy for academic achievement, being in the top percentile in the State for several strands of the NAPLAN National Assessment Program's standardised tests. At seven, she asked me to explain the "missing links" in the Theory of Evolution. My response was, "Go ask your father." As a teenage girl, she produced essays equivalent to third-year literary theory university papers.

At 15, her essays in Year 10 were often described by her teachers as challenging to mark because the standard was so high they had no metric to grade them. Of course, she got an A+ in English, but teachers said she deserved a *higher* grade! The point is that every special needs child has a special gift. Some kids have low-functioning autism and are music or art prodigies.

Our daughter was diagnosed as a savant in the areas of both literary art (writing) and fine art (drawing). She began drawing at a very young age, spending hours scribbling little, beady-eyed phantoms on her whiteboard, to which she would flap her arms excitedly, delighted with her creations. She was the youngest child accepted into the gifted artist program at her primary (elementary) school. She won a real estate company's first national art competition at six. At 15, she was awarded the "highly commended artist" prize in Staedtler's National Annual Artist competition. To this day, she remains a fantastic animal portrait artist, as you can see below, with two examples of her incredible work. She can also paint and change her artistic style depending on her mood.

Our daughter's pencil sketches of a Labrador dog, and our brindle Persian cat, completed at the age of 15.

Our 12-year-old ASD son can also sketch very well and has an incredible talent for sculpting clay and Fimo figurines. He has spent hours watching clay-modelling YouTube videos and re-created the works with his own hands. I learned early on that it is vital to discover and nurture your child's gifts and focus on their strengths. Your special child deals with many life battles, such as poor communication and social skills, so their blessed gift must be encouraged and developed to build their self-esteem.

Our daughter has the natural ability to visualise virtual worlds in her mind because of DID, which is familiar to people who have this disorder. When experiencing a trigger that causes significant distress, our daughter's brain switches from the core personality to another 'part' as a form of protection. Fascinated by all this, I asked her where she goes when she disappears. She told me that sometimes she remembers nothing at all. On other occasions, she goes to her inner world. Ruby told me that the inner world is an internal mind-scape where her alters interact. They live in a Victorian mansion surrounded by beautiful gardens, and each alter has a bedroom decorated to their taste. There is a skateboarding half-pipe in the front yard for Edmund, who is learning to skate. On one particularly memorable occasion, I recall entertaining a 16-year-old alter named Juliet for over 24 hours: she had a British accent and explained that her function was to help Ruby. When our daughter's core personality returned, I informed her of how upsetting the whole episode was for me.

Each alter has a specific function designated by the brain to help Ruby cope. For example, Edmund's role is that of a protector, and so he typically presents when our daughter is feeling vulnerable to harming herself. I would often tell my daughter that her 'natural' lived experience is much like what the technology companies are attempting to create with Virtual Reality. Electronic devices allow people to escape into artificial, dream-like worlds. This ability to dissociate and enter her very own personal VR world is something you expect to see written in a comic book or a science fiction movie. Still, people who have Dissociative Identity Disorder do this involuntarily. Unfortunately, DID characters are often disparaged in literary fiction and movies: our daughter once commented that people with DID are portrayed as psychos and serial killers. I would love to see the end of such depictions as they stigmatise people with DID and create stereotypes that are harmful. This can have a direct impact on family members or friends when they are informed that their loved ones have this disorder.

What is not readily known is that people with DID, when accessing the right treatment, can live relatively normal lives. Because of social stigma however, their perception of who they are instantly changes after diagnosis. Due to a lack of knowledge and poor media representation of this disorder, some family members might conclude the child is crazy and should be confined to a medical facility. In some cases, they might even believe the child is demonically possessed and requires exorcism!

Some people believe that DID isn't a real condition and that the child is pretending to have the disorder in order to manipulate their parents and gain attention or get their own way. Many marriages, friendships, and families suffer due to a lack of understanding about these children's disabilities. When your child is first diagnosed with a neurodivergent condition, consider finding a superhero with whom they can relate, and ensure you have representations of that hero in their bedroom, such as posters, plush toys, action figures, and branded merchandise. Encourage them to watch superhero cartoons with you and compare the hero's life with your child's: the ups and downs, The good and the bad, warts and all.

Another idea is to spend more time with people who are supportive of your child's disability and less time with people who don't understand your child's health issues, because your child's self-esteem will suffer under constant negativity. We decided a couple of years ago not to have anything more to do with two family members because of their ignorance and arrogance, which had already caused much pain to our small family. Sometimes, we have to cut family members from our lives, as our daughter's paediatric psychiatrist advised us we needed to form a protective barrier around our children and altogether remove from our lives those who pose a threat to our children's mental health.

My father is the inspiration for my tenacity, and he is my superhero. At the tender age of 21, he had his right leg amputated because of a severe work-related injury he sustained on the Snowy Mountains Hydro-electricity Scheme. I have many fond memories of my dad making me laugh as he pretended his stump was a dog and made barking noises. He would piggyback me to bed until I was seven years old and take me swimming every Saturday. He didn't care about the reaction of onlookers when he took his prosthetic leg off to go into the water. In the playground at my local primary school, I would tell other children that my dad was more remarkable than the other kids' dads because he could take his leg off anytime. My dad taught me that it is okay to be different.

Over the years, I have come to understand that the most common mistake that parents of special needs children make is trying to get their kids to fit in with their neurotypical peers. Whilst this is an understandable ideal, be warned that there will always be kids who will be mean to your child simply because they are different. When your children are upset about not being invited to someone's birthday party or they're treated terribly at school, I like to ask my children, "Why fit in when you were born to stand out?"

Our children are exceptional and extraordinarily gifted, so they need to be proud of being different. However, the natural desire of all kids to 'fit in' and be accepted by their peers makes instilling such confident self-assurance somewhat problematic. Constant praise is needed to remind your child of their intrinsic worth, especially when they come home crying and wishing they were 'normal'. What is normal anyway? We are all born unique and different from everyone else: different ethnicities, cultures, views, morals, characteristics, likes, and dislikes. We are all made differently for a reason, just like our fingerprints; no other person will have identical prints.

Like comic superheroes, your child also has strengths and weaknesses. Focus on their strengths for positive reinforcement and spend less time on the skills they need to be proficient in, such as stuttering or poor coordination. Specialists such as occupational therapists and psychologists can address these issues more effectively. Your child needs to find their own 'tribe' of like-minded people, which may take a while, so please be persistent and patient. Our son's closest friends tend to be a little younger than he is. He enjoys spending time with them and works hard to set a good example. Our daughter's tribe is a group of old-school friends and other teens with health issues. They are so accepting of her, and each friend complements her differently. Making friends in small towns can be challenging, so involvement in special needs groups is essential even if you must travel outside your area to join these social groups.

Keeping a visual diary of your child's positive experiences, complete with photos and dates, can cheer them up when they have a bad day and feel rejected. Mothers of special needs children also need to find *their* tribe: a supportive group of parents in similar circumstances who can relate to what they're going through. They should be a non-judgmental sounding board for downloading each other's concerns in an accepting spirit of cooperation and encouragement. Sometimes, even one good and understanding friend can make all the difference, and I am blessed to have my beautiful friend, my oracle Ceils. Owing to her experiences with autism in her own family, she knew my kids were autistic and subtly encouraged me to get them tested. She remains a constant inspiration and is always there for me when I need her. So don't despair. Your little superhero is destined to achieve great things. All they need is love, a great costume, and encouragement from you – their teacher and mentor – to inspire them to adopt a superhero mentality daily.

CHAPTER 3
WHY FIT IN WHEN YOU WERE MEANT TO STAND OUT

My dad taught me that it is okay to be different. He would always be in trouble playing practical jokes on workmates, such as painting a bunch of cane toads and Christmas wrapping them in a big box with a false bottom, finished with a big bow. He gave this memorable gift to the lunch ladies at work, and their mortified expressions were priceless when the bottom gave way, and 30 brightly coloured cane toads escaped the box and wound up jumping all around the lunch room. The women were hysterical, jumping up on tables to get away from the wart-skinned army. Those lovely ladies chased my dad around the cafeteria with a wet mop. He well deserved any swats the ladies landed on him.

My dad is a perfect example of an Aussie larrikin, which means he is a practical joker who is well-liked by others, and this despite having a missing limb. He doesn't let that missing limb prevent him from climbing to the top of my family's A-framed house, and it was common to see him up there in howling winds during cyclone season, wearing a bright yellow raincoat and rain pelting his face as he shut the top windows to oncoming storms. I often worried he might fly off in the wind like Dorothy in The Wizard Of Oz. My sister and I used to play our practical jokes on dad, hiding his artificial leg or unscrewing the detachable foot and adding marbles to it so that he would rattle as he walked. He always had a great sense of humour regarding our antics and took our pranks on the chin.

I never fitted in with the other kids at school, and although I had one dear friend as a child, I didn't have any close friends at high school. Kids are mean, and your child will be made fun of and taunted at least at some point in their lives, if not often, for not being like the children who inflict these torments. Your child's strengths and weaknesses will weed out those who aren't meant to be in their lives. My daughter only has a handful of childhood friends, but they are accepting and supportive of her daily struggles and love her different DID personalities. I have often told their mums what terrific kids they have raised and how blessed my daughter is to have them in their lives.

Once our daughter was old enough to go out with her friends and legally drink alcohol (18 years of age in Australia), we discovered an interesting effect: when her alters got tipsy, she would sober up when Ruby, her leading personality, returned. Though I wouldn't give her a police breath test, it is amazing how the brain acts when different parts front. This is an example of how it's okay to be different, so I ask: why fit in when you're meant to stand out?

We moved to a country town about seven years ago for a slower pace of life and a soothing 'tree change.' Unfortunately, our daughter hasn't found new friends here, so she regularly spends time with her childhood friends who live in the city we left, an hour away. Because their social skills can be pretty poor, and yet they are eager to fit in and will do almost anything for friendship, kids on the Spectrum typically have a hard time at mainstream schools and are often easy targets for bullies. For example, some boys at kindy dared my son to perform outrageously rude stunts. Being ignorant of social norms and expectations, he did as they asked, thinking he could win over these boys who were, in fact, maliciously humiliating him.

After years of witnessing our daughter being bullied at both public and private schools, our son's experience at kindergarten forced our decision to homeschool him from the outset. It is vital to be aware of your child's social interactions, whether positive or negative. Unfortunately, bullying has caused a lot of psychological damage to our eldest child, which we are still working through with therapists a decade later.

Years ago, I realised that God made me a quirky and outside-of-the-box thinker, so why should I pretend to be someone I'm not? I can recall that as a teenager, I was bullied by never being invited to parties. Other girls never understood me, and I wasn't interested in their gossip about boys anyway. I had always wanted to be a radio journalist and planned to attend university in Sydney. I created quite a stir at our high school prom night by wearing a velvet tuxedo instead of a dress. I no longer cared what the other girls thought of me by this time. I liked how I looked and felt comfortable on the night; that was more important than fitting in with the other teens.

The girls in high school were not friendly at all. There were three groups: the popular girls, the sometimes fit-in girls, and the outcasts. I preferred the last group as they were the most creative and had unusual ideas about life, especially music. I also tended to gravitate towards boys rather than girls as friends. The boys were loyal and weren't interested in backstabbing like most of the teenage girls were. Because I grew up in a country town in North Queensland with only one radio station, accessing New Wave music from England and bands like Joy Division, New Order, and The Cure was difficult. The boys I befriended ordered records from Brisbane, and it was very exciting to hear refreshingly 'real' music. After graduating high school, I relocated to Sydney to study Journalism and Creative Writing.

Finally, free of parental constraints, I could experiment with my looks, mess with my hair and makeup, buy amazing pre-loved clothes from opportunity (thrift) shops, and go to alternative music nightclubs in the city.

When I went home to visit family over Christmas vacations, I found it amusing that the high school kids who used to ridicule me behind my back now wanted to be my friends. Back in the early '90s, it was unusual to see someone with coloured hair in my hometown, but in Sydney, a friend and I frequented a punk shop to buy small tubs of outlandishly coloured hair dye that was imported from England. Nowadays, brightly coloured hair dye is available at any local supermarket, and it's common to see people sporting unnaturally coloured hair. But back then, my appearance was quite scandalous in my hometown's local night spots. I even had an eighteen-year-old boy experimenting with Goth fashion present me with a handwritten poem expressing his admiration for me. His name was Robert, and we became friends. This kind gesture was part of the healing in my heart from the bullying I endured in high school.

I was finally comfortable in my new skin, a black-clothed, dark-haired youth who was finally learning that it was okay to be different. University was a fantastic time for me; the bizarre parties are fixed in my memory even 30 years later, especially an incident involving Bunty, the punk rocker and two schooners of beer. My close friend Lesley and I were at The Swamp Bar – the university's watering hole – near closing time at nine when alcohol service had stopped for the night. However, in the centre of the room, seated at a small table bristling with full glasses of beer, was a large man with a purple mohawk, tattoos, and a studded leather jacket.

Leaving me to approach him, Lesley whispered something in his ear. When they looked in my direction, and he smiled a toothless grin, I was immediately concerned about what they might be scheming. Lesley came over, took me by my hand and dragged me to this ominous-looking individual. Pushing me onto his lap, she said, "Sonia, meet Bunty. Bunty, this is Sonia!" as his giant arms encased me. Lesley then took two beers, retreated to the corner of the room where we were initially seated, and grinned cheekily at me. The man informed me that my best friend was given two beers in exchange for an introduction to me. I was going to get even with her for this because before I escaped, I discovered that punk rocker Bunty had just been released from prison for aggravated assault!

Lesley apologised, but I knew she was watching from a distance to ensure my safety. But Bunty appeared at an Enid Blyton party after the Swamp Bar closed. Lesley and I took a cab to the party, and you can imagine my alarm at arriving to see Bunty, whom I had ditched only hours before, drunk as a skunk outside the party house, chasing four Goth boys down the street with a broken wooden chair! It was like witnessing a scene from the British comedy *The Young Ones* with punk rocker Vivian running amok.

I 'found myself' at university, and from experimenting with my appearance in the world, I gained knowledge that would, in the then-distant future, become invaluable when parenting my daughter. I look at this carefree period with great affection as I met my husband of over 26 years at this time. I still love alternative '80s music and op-shop-sourced clothing. I now also revamp old wooden furniture, mixing stained and polished wood pieces with distressed, chalk-white 'shabby-chic' treatments that I apply to add to my home's provincial, country-inspired decor. I am a landscape artist and a writer, and I love gardening and baking. At 51, I am finally comfortable with who I am. It was a long journey getting here, but two essential rules inform my witty and fun-loving demeanour around our family: Always be honest and straightforward with your kids and act like an oddball with a good sense of humour. That's how we can also navigate tricky social settings in the real world.

I want to set an example of Christian motherhood to my children by treating others with kindness, including strangers. Calling someone in a shop by their first name takes little effort. You will see their faces light up when you do this. Performing kind gestures for others is a way we can show that we care. I don't want to be a condemning Christian but rather one who demonstrates their faith through acts of kindness that will leave a lasting impression on the recipient and on my children. I often give our support workers home-baked goods and take an interest in their personal lives. There is not enough kindness in the world, as everyone seems to be focused on their worldly pleasures instead of putting other people's needs before their own, which is a fundamental Biblical principle. So, fitting in is overrated for me, and I have now become a partial recluse, focusing on my family and trying to be the best wife and mother I can be. I don't need to belong to a group of female friends who go to dinner parties, restaurants, or cafes to catch up on gossip and compare themselves with others. I'm not interested in travelling overseas, as I think that travel money does far more good being donated to charities helping in third-world countries. But that is just my personal opinion.

Ensure your child understands that they were born amazingly gifted and that being different is good. It may take time to discover their gifts, such as the arts or sciences, but they will be revealed as a special aptitude or passion that you can help grow to ignite their soul. Your children will get to where they were meant to be socially and work-wise. If you have faith that God is with you in all the trials you endure, you and your family will triumph. It just takes time and patience. Remember the story about the rabbit and the tortoise? The tortoise won the race at a slow but steady pace. This, too, will happen to your kids.

CHAPTER 4
KEEP THE FAITH

Thanks to my father, I always believed in God. He encouraged me to go to church with him twice on Sundays. Unbeknownst to my proud Catholic mum, my dad rewarded my attendance with him at church with jam and cream doughnuts. I prayed before bed and was aware from near-death experiences, such as nearly getting hit by a car outside our church at eight years of age, that there was a higher power watching over me.

My faith is an essential tool in my Crazy Mother's survival kit. There have been plenty of times when I was emotionally drained and had to take a shower, letting the water wash away my tears and fears. Mums are familiar with feeling overloaded, wanting to pack a suitcase and leave the house with the front door swinging in their wake. You want a break; you need a break from the mounting stress of solving bizarre problems. Let's face it: mums must be as resourceful and adaptable as Swiss Army knives: multiple tools in one! We must wear many hats in the family home: chef, nurse, therapist, cleaner, grocery shopper, lover to our partner and an attentive mother to our children. There is even an expectation for modern mothers to work a job or financially contribute to the family in some way. It is exhausting, and that is where my faith in Jesus Christ comes into play. I am not ashamed to talk about my faith; it is why I am still alive.

I also battled severe suicidal depression and mental health issues in my late teens and early adulthood. The last serious episode of severe suicidal depression was when I was pregnant with my son, and it was due to the hormones raging inside my body as God was slowly knitting together the precious cargo in the safety of my womb. It was a distressing time when I was eight months pregnant, battling crippling suicidal ideation and suffering from insomnia. There were two instances when I woke up standing next to my bed. I don't remember getting up, but I was undoubtedly frightened to wake in the dark of night, upright beside my bed. It had never happened before, nor since.

After our baby boy was born, I suffered post-natal depression. I know what it is like to be on the shower floor crying for your world to end. I felt like the waves of life were crashing down all around me, engulfing my sanity. I pleaded with God, begging for answers regarding the suicidal depression as I couldn't take it anymore. He answered my prayer two days later when I was diagnosed with Premenstrual Dysphoric Disorder (PMDD) by a gynaecologist. This is a severe form of Premenstrual Syndrome (PMS) that causes suicidal depression every period cycle. I came very close to suicide quite a few times. For example, I had to finish my undergraduate university studies at home, under the careful supervision of my psychiatrist.

The reason I am discussing mental health issues is because there is a high risk of hormone-induced, severe suicidal depression and anxiety in ASD kids (especially girls) when they reach puberty. Before our daughter turned 13, I was advised by her doctor to see a gynaecologist who specialised in treating ASD girls for severe hormonal issues associated with their menstrual cycles. I was told that a majority of teenage autistic girls develop severe mental health issues because of PMDD. If your teenage autistic daughter is battling mental health issues and depression, and you notice it happens cyclically around the time of her period, please pay attention to that and act accordingly. Another prominent symptom of PMDD is if her mental health improves after her period. These are signs that it may be worthwhile investigating whether she has PMDD or other gynaecological issues.

I know what it's like to feel trapped in a cave of despair, not knowing when you will turn a corner in the tunnel and open onto a sunlit meadow. I am a proud Christian mum who understood that God accepted and loved me as I am from the outset. My whole problem was that I took myself too seriously instead of accepting myself for the harmless cracker that I am. I have learnt to accept myself because my Creator – the Creator of the universe – has accepted me! I am an oddball, and it took a long time for me to understand that Christians come in many different shapes and sizes, which is how God designed us, and He doesn't make mistakes.

A few years ago, I asked my kids to buy me a Mister Potato Head doll because my mum wouldn't let me have one when I was a child. Our gorgeous teenage girl surprised me with a collection of Potato Heads and accessories for my birthday. I was so excited because I now had these dolls proudly displayed on my desk; one looked just like my dad, and the other very much like my mother!

As with school, I don't fit into that conservative, cookie-cutter Christian mould, and unfortunately, my family has been badly burnt in the past by gossip and slanderers at church, so I no longer try to put on airs and graces. How was I saved? My husband had much to do with my salvation as he was pretty unusual and odd, had fantastic taste in '80s music and had an amazing heart. I met him at university in the '90s, and we were close friends before we started dating. He readily emptied his wallet to needy people asking him for a handout when we went out in Sydney, which tugged at my heartstrings. I now know that God brought him into my life because we are two oddballs who would one day have a clan of Christian oddballs. We are an artistic family of musicians, visual artists, and writers.

My husband is a talented musician who produces music under the name *Beautiful Desert*. He was involved in the Australian

Punk Rock, New Wave and Goth scene, embracing the alternative music sounds primarily emanating from England in the late 1970s and early 1980s. He was particularly excited by English bands like Joy Division / New Order, Bauhaus, The Cure, and he is very knowledgeable about alternative '70s and '80s music and culture. He has seen many of these fantastic artists perform live, in their prime.

This intimate knowledge and love of the '80s alternative musical broad sound is echoed in his original songs. The music was composed in the '80s, and he has since added Biblical lyrics to that music as he works to produce a home-recorded album. It's grungy, melodic music that also ministers about the saving power of Jesus' work on the cross. I am so proud of what he has achieved, and he has encouraged me to write our family story as parents of special needs kids. Partnering with me in parenting our special kids has been his priority, so his musical pursuits must often take a backseat to the demands of family life. God has the perfect timing for everything. We don't realise He builds character, patience, and endurance to release our creativity at an unknown time. We need to seek God and wait on His calling. I encourage you to check out the link to my husband's Christian music ministry in the Social Media section at the end of this book.

I want to share an intimate spiritual experience that has rocked me. Three years ago, I went to my doctor to have him check a small spot on my arm. A punch biopsy resulted in my being called back to the doctor's office to be told that it was a spot of aggressive melanoma skin cancer, and I was immediately referred to a skin cancer clinic at a major hospital. He said, "I'm sorry." I left the office in a daze as my world crumbled around me, not knowing if I would be alive in a year.

When I got home, I called a close doctor friend and told her what had occurred. I can never repay her kindness as she comforted and reassured me, telling me not to worry and that I could count on her support. At this time, the cancer wasn't staged, as I needed to have the spot excised for testing. I also had lymph nodes removed to determine whether the melanoma had spread beyond that spot on my arm. Since I was having surgery, I wanted to know with a greater degree of certainty what was going on inside my body. But what was happening to me spiritually was quite another thing altogether.

I was frightened and confused, and as any mum can imagine when you are given a cancer diagnosis – be it melanoma, breast cancer or ovarian cancer – the first thought that runs through your mind is: *Am I going to see my children grow up?* My special needs kids need me; I need them, and most importantly, my husband – who is the love of my life – needs me. I had to wait a month for surgery and during that time, I would spontaneously burst into tears as I pondered my life and the future.

Within a week of being told the bad news, I went to my bedroom mirror and cut my long, wavy hair to a shoulder-length bob. A great mass of burgundy strands collected at my feet, and I gazed into the mirror, relieved by the results of my cathartic self-therapy. It was as if I could physically remove the cancer by shedding my hair. But at that point, I remembered who could remove the tumour, and staring into the mirror, I said, "God, I hand this situation over to you; I love you and leave my life in your hands." A peace came over me as I felt God's presence and reassurance that He had the situation in hand; all I needed to do was to cling to His promises and ride out this catastrophe. During this time, I sometimes woke up early and burst into tears. Whilst sleeping, my mind was processing the gravity of the situation and producing fear and trepidation for the future. But something strange happened while waiting for the surgery date: on two occasions, a flash of white light filled my bedroom as I slowly drifted back to sleep after going to the bathroom late at night. I then felt an intense heat on the area of my arm where the melanoma was. This happened twice and is an integral part of this true life story.

The excision surgery happened three weeks after the last of these 'spiritual experiences,' and the area around the melanoma spot was removed and sent for testing, as were the three lymph nodes (sentinel glands) from my right armpit. It would be a couple of weeks before I received the results, but as I was lying in recovery at the hospital, I lifted my hospital gown and noticed that my upper chest area was utterly black from bruising. This would earn me the title of 'Black Booby Mama' by my clever son when I arrived home from the hospital. No, I didn't show him; he just overheard my discussion with my husband in the kitchen. As you may know, ASD kids have hearing like a Canine: the walls have ears! You can be in any room in your house, and they will hear you. A week after convalescing at home from surgery, the sore in my armpit where I had those glands removed, started to ooze blood and pus, and I developed a high fever.

I was rushed to my local (rural) hospital with a nasty infection and then transported back to the metropolitan hospital, where I had the initial surgery to undergo intravenous antibiotic treatment. Every six hours, I was given life-saving medicine to combat the infection, circulated through an IV drip attached to the central vein in my arm. After a week of treatment, both my arms were bruised black from the insertion and removal of cannulas. I honestly looked like a drug addict with all the needle tracks up my arms.

On the last day of my hospital stay, the specialist Plastic Surgeon treating me visited with a team of young medical students. He explained my medical history and then had me stand up next to the windows and turn around slowly to show the students how bad the bruising on my chest was. It didn't matter to him that I was giving the whole city a ready view of my black boobs as I was asked to stand close to the windows to bathe my wounds in natural light.

As I put my gown back on, my surgeon dismissed the medical students and then explained the final results of the melanoma excision to me, saying, "I want you to know that your particular case has been very intriguing." He was busy looking at his clipboard and reviewing the medical notes as he spoke, and with great apprehension, I braced myself for the worst regarding the staging of the cancer. He looked up from his clipboard and said, "We have never had a case like yours."

"What do you mean?" I asked, flustered and bewildered by what the doctor was trying to say.

"You don't have cancer," he said.

"What? I don't understand," I responded.

The doctor then clarified that he had two meetings with other medical professionals about my case and redid the original bloodwork from the punch biopsy. He explained that the original test confirmed there was a cancer spot, but when they tested the removed chunk of flesh that made my arm resemble that of a shark attack victim, there were no cancerous cells at all in there! I was in shock. He then explained that the only conclusion the medical team could come up with was that the cancer was caught just as it started: it was entirely removed in the punch biopsy performed a month before my surgery!

I felt peace come over me, and I said, "That's not what happened."

"What do you mean?" the doctor asked quizzically.

"God cured me!" I declared passionately, remembering the flashes of white light and the warm sensation over my arm on those two occasions when I prayed for healing. I now believe that light was an angel sent by God to heal me, and I have a strong witness as to how powerfully God answers prayer. He may not always give us what we ask for, but sometimes He does.

Regardless of how He responds, we must believe and trust God in all our circumstances and lean on Him in difficult times. I have been so blessed to have an extraordinary minister and his family in our lives for over 27 years. When my husband and I relocated to Queensland after completing our university studies in Sydney, we worked through a marriage preparation course with our pastor, Chris J. His austere facade when I first met him soon dissolved as he could see that hubby and I were casual, accepting people who believed that light-hearted humour and generosity of spirit would be effective devices for navigating married life. The Baptist church he had just started ministering at wasn't quite ready for the Chris J. *Evolution Of Ministers Tour Show* he brought to proceedings: he was an outside-of-the-box thinker. Chris was refreshingly 'real' and unpretentious, a down-to-earth bloke who was trustworthy, knowledgeable and dependable. He reminded me of that one incredible teacher in school that we all looked up to: intelligent, charismatic, and hip enough that you can both respect and feel at ease around them and learn from them. That is what Chris J. is like.

No ordinary minister: Chris is a Ramones fan, for goodness sake! I had never met a Pastor with great taste in music. He officiated our wedding and made a real impact at our wedding ceremony by using a Star Trek illustration to make a point during the obligatory *How to get along with your spouse* sermon. I loved that. Such a quirky, folksy and memorable touch! I have always gravitated to people who dance to a different tune. This minister has shown me that I could accept myself as God had made me and stop trying to be something I wasn't.

Chris and his gorgeous wife have been in our lives for a long time, and though they moved away decades ago, we still keep in contact and often watch his sermons on YouTube. He is the most relaxed minister I know, and his discussion of Star Trek during our wedding made me appreciate him all the more because of his individuality. I still remember the tortured expression my Catholic mum pulled at the mere mention of Star Trek. Years later, she still rants about how it wasn't appropriate in a wedding sermon. I believe my mum has PTSL: Post-Traumatic Sermon Listener! Chris is my Obi-Wan and has supported our family since our married life journey started. He has instructed me when to use the Lightsaber and when to use The Force.

So why is Faith an essential tool for surviving being a parent of special needs kids? A relationship with God will keep you going, especially during tough times. I have often called my Obi-Wan for spiritual advice and comfort during difficult parenting situations. Over the years, I have learned that when I encounter the storms of life, Jesus calms the raging seas that threaten to overwhelm me.

It is difficult to find a church that is good with special needs kids, as many church members don't understand or even believe that your children's neurodivergent behaviours are the result of an actual medical condition. So you must be flexible and patient as you persevere, trying out different churches until you find one where your children are accepted and happy. It may take a while, and thanks to COVID-19, thousands of churches began posting their services online during the lockdowns, so now you can enjoy church services from the comfort of your home while you look for your 'spiritual home.' We have called online church attendance 'bed church' since the COVID-19 lockdowns when our family and pets piled onto our bed and snuggled under the doona to watch our Zoomed church services.

We must realise and accept that we are only human, and when trouble comes, it is okay to have days that aren't okay. These are the days I cling to my faith and pray. I pray for resolutions to my parenting problems. I pray for our kids' lives to get sorted so our little boat travels on calm waters, not stormy seas. Most importantly, I pray because I want to maintain my intimate connection with the supreme Creator of the universe whose Son died on the cross for me!

As the saying goes, *Rome wasn't built in a day!* It seems unfair when your family goes through hard times because of your child's disabilities, and it is okay to be angry that your precious child was born with special needs. The frustration can build to where you might feel that you can't handle another severe family crisis, but to be honest, this is very common in special needs families. So, release all the inner pain and anger in healthy ways. Use it to get housework done or to exercise, for example.

Close to her 16th birthday, our daughter had given up hope, but I am blessed to have a wonderful friend who organised an action plan. She invited our family and two of our daughter's closest friends to holiday with her on the coast for a weekend away from home. The whole purpose of the trip was to 'reset' our home life with a relaxing, carefree pause from the heaviness of our situation. Such 'resets' are essential when your child feels genuinely overwhelmed. Removing them from the dowdiness of familiar surroundings to an exciting place, like the beachside apartment we stayed in, and enjoying some time away and having fun can be just the ticket. It could be a family weekend away or an overnight stay with a trusted family member: get them away from their home environment. Our family, particularly our daughter and her friends, had a fabulous time celebrating her 16th birthday.

The highlight of the weekend was a frighteningly realistic 'brain' cake consisting of a lump of marzipan tubes covered in red food colouring – its appearance expertly crafted by our fantastic doctor friend. When I am having a tough day with my daughter, I often look at a photo of her smiling radiantly, flanked by her beaming friends, all proudly gathered around that 'brain' birthday cake.

Our daughter made it through her 16th birthday, a significant accomplishment. But being a mum who knows her mental health can change quickly, I knew she wasn't out of the woods yet. With daily trepidation, I checked in on my daughter every morning and then, depending on her mood, planned the rest of the day accordingly.

CHAPTER 5
DEF-CON ONE

There is nothing more distressing than holding your child as they talk about taking their own life. At that moment, one feels helpless, exhausted and unsure of what to do as a mother and caregiver. If you have supported your child through a mental health crisis, from personal experience battling such crises in my late teens, I can tell you the worst thing you can say to them is, "Get over it!" There's no magical cure for mental health.

Spiritual elements beyond our control are at play in suicidal ideation and depression, exacerbating personal tragedies. God is the only answer to stopping nuclear detonations during these 'Def-Con One' moments when the red 'self-destruct' buttons are being pushed. I have been in this situation with my daughter many times and want to share some personal advice with other parents currently walking this treacherous path alone. Your child can get through this horrific day, but they need you to be the one guiding them to the light. The following are some helpful tactics

I have developed during my spiritual quest as a mother to my extraordinary but fragile kids.

Crises happened too often in my house. I have all the emergency phone numbers at hand. I have all our medications locked away in a box. I have a sedative at hand, prescribed by Ruby's doctors to calm her down when needed. Our daughter is susceptible to the various medications we have tried over the years, but we found one that she didn't have side effects with. A low dose of this medication is administered at the first sign of severe distress. My advice for parents under these circumstances includes:

1. Use after-hours crisis lines. They are staffed by helpful counsellors who are trained in suicide prevention.
2. All medicines should be locked in a box, and the key should be hidden in a separate area of the house.
3. Ensure you child-proof your house by hiding away cleaning products, kitchen knives and scissors, razors and especially ropes and belts.
4. Be realistic. It is impossible to remove every threat, but you want to make it difficult for your child to access these items during periods of emotional distress.

5. When your child leaves the house, encourage someone to be with them and watch what harmful objects they can bring home without your knowledge. You need to be aware that sometimes the child hides these implements for self-harm outside until they can find a moment to smuggle them inside without your detection.
6. You have every right to search their room for hidden implements for self-harm. Search blankets and doonas in cupboards as I have found implements wrapped tightly inside.
7. Completing a CPR and First Aid course, usually run by your local ambulance organisation, would be helpful.
8. Ensure your First Aid kit is up-to-date with disinfectant, bandages, and especially Steri-Strips: stronger than bandaids, these thin adhesive strips clamp wounds together when you can't get to a medical facility. Please note that this only applies to deeper but non-life-threatening cuts, and seeing a doctor as soon as possible afterwards is essential. These stitch-like, zipper bandages will help if you live in a rural location and medical facilities aren't open until morning.

9. During bouts of suicidal depression, your child needs to be monitored carefully. Fix your child something to eat and a warm drink, as this will help distract and calm the emotionally distraught youngster, giving them time to collect their thoughts and apply some reasoning again. I always have my children's favourite snacks at hand for emergency situations.

10. Stay with your child until they are asleep. I am a light sleeper, so I stayed beside her and watched movies on the couch. I am like a watchdog; it doesn't take much for me to wake up. You must remain in the same room with your child until the threat has passed.

11. Use chamomile tea and lavender oil; use whatever calming herbal and essential oils you can to provide a relaxing environment to help your child regulate their emotions. I don't exclude mainstream medical interventions at all. The light sedative previously mentioned is locked away in my medicine box to be used only on those occasions when our daughter is at risk of self-harming.

12. Have an 'emergency' person who understands your situation and is willing to look after your other kids whilst you rush

your child to the hospital. This individual or individuals needs to be prepared to support you during the early hours of the morning. Unfortunately, after-hours visits to the hospital seem to be very common when you have a suicidal teen. There is nothing worse than having to drag all your children along with you, and it is also traumatic for them.

13. If your child's condition hasn't settled within a few hours of medication, take them to the nearest emergency department. Be prepared for a long wait; the induction nurse will watch over them.

14. When the crisis is over, ask family or friends to come and mind your child/children while you recover from the ordeal. You must destress and catch up on sleep, but your child can't be left unattended.

So, my advice as a 'crazy mother' is to take each day as it comes: the good and the bad. On the bad days, I tend to cling to my children's achievements as I yearn for the darkness to pass and the glorious sunrise to dawn on a brand new day. We're only human, and it's okay to feel suffocated and gasping for air at times. It is essential to stop panicking and remember to breathe. To take the edge off a panic attack, spend time in prayer, listen to music and participate in relaxation techniques such as slow breathing and meditating on God's word.

When you're in the thick of these battles with darkness, remember to look for the life preserver that God will throw to you, but you need to look for it. The life preserver can be your partner, your parents, a close family friend, a mentor or another parent with special needs children who know exactly what you're going through and will listen to you non-judgmentally. But most importantly, my primary life preserver is Jesus Christ. In times of trouble, He is our greatest friend and comforter.

CHAPTER 6
FILTER FILTER FILTER

If there is one word I must say over a hundred times a day, it is 'filter.' When I say this, I am a verbal reminder for my kids, especially our teenage boy, to stop and think about the inappropriate sentences or words they have said.

What is it with boys and body parts? Our son is 12, but even a few years ago, he looked for any excuse to flash his body parts because he thought it was funny. When he was younger, our would-be Man Power entertainer loved to run up and down the hallway in his underwear and a paper bag on his head with holes cut out for his eyes – a bizarre adaptation of the bushranger Ned Kelly's famous outfit. My best friend told me it is normal for boys at this age to be obsessed with their genitalia, but coming from a family of all female siblings, I was somewhat uncomfortable with this obsession. Our beautiful daughter has her moments, too. There is a seven-year age gap between the two kids because I was afraid of being pregnant again after my first child was born, being wary of the potential health risks as I had severe blood pressure issues and permanent damage to my right foot from an epidural from my first pregnancy.

It was 12 years ago when I was up all night with my fevered infant son. I had just put him down in his bouncer when 'little Miss know-it-all' woke up and decided to grace me with her presence. She was seven at the time, and after examining her crying baby brother, she turned to me and suggested, "Why don't you be a good mother and pick up your crying child?" as she went into her bedroom to ready herself for school. I burst into tears because I had only put him down five minutes earlier, sleep-deprived from staying up with the boy half the night, and now this little smarty pants was judging me.

Our daughter is a real-life Wednesday Addams. She may have had long, strawberry-blonde hair when this incident happened, but when she got older, she dyed her hair in many colours, including jet black. At 19, she still wears her Goth clothes, but when she was nine, a boy at church tried to impress her with his Pekingese puppy dog. Ruby was minding her own business when this blonde-headed boy approached her and, with a cheeky smile, said, "You know, I can get my dog to attack you." Mildly annoyed, she looked at him and calmly replied, "Did you know that if you hold and squeeze a Pekingese a certain way, you can get their eyeballs to pop out? Here, let me show you …" she said as she motioned to take the dog into her arms. The poor boy went pale and quickly left her presence, clinging to his dog tightly. I watched the interaction closely: she didn't smile and walked away in the opposite direction.

Pekingese dogs' eyeballs can readily pop out because their protruding eyeballs are set into tiny eye sockets. "Ruby, what was all that about?" I inquired. She gave me a cheeky smile and responded, "Don't worry, Mum, I just wanted to scare him." You see, she heard a conversation I had with her father a few weeks earlier about a family friend who used to breed these dogs professionally. I mentioned to my husband that the eyes are a significant problem with this breed. My little genius locked that information away in her memory and decided to use it to shock that poor boy.

Our son is the family court jester and always seems to break the ice with a ludicrously bizarre quip or stunt when we are experiencing some severe mental health incident with our oldest child. He has the best sense of humour and comes up with the most unhinged, hilarious one-liners. He often utters such nonsense at dinner, sending food spitting out of my mouth as I gasp for air, wrong-footed and abruptly launched into a bout of hysterical laughter.

When he was three, we went to a carnival and he and his older sister went on a giant slide. They were up at the top of the slide with their mats when I saw the ride operator talking to my son, and then looking down towards me, he burst into laughter. I was instantly suspicious that my son's 'no filter' mouth was at work. When he and his sister slid down the Big Dipper, my daughter ran to me, laughing and out of breath. "Mum! Mum! You wouldn't believe what Robert said to the slide operator!" I knew instantly that this wouldn't be good. "He told that man that his mum had a great set of boobs!" Well, that explained the man's reaction, and of course, my face instantly turned red.

Robert's inappropriate comments can sometimes be offensive, so his therapists are currently working with him on this issue. They are trying to teach him proper etiquette, situational awareness and appropriate modes of communication. But hardly a day goes by when my husband and I are not in hysterics about something our son says. One of our son's most memorable compliments was, "Mum, you are so much better than the other trampy mums in the area." I didn't know whether to take it as a compliment or an insult, as he was technically implying that I am trampy, just not as trampy as others. The joys of having no filter!

How does one correct these gorgeous little souls who say the most inappropriate things at the worst times? Unfortunately, it requires a lot of therapy and parental lectures over a long period, which requires patience from the parents. Still, we don't want to crush their creativity and unique personalities. Guided by our God-given sense of humour, we can pick our battles, allowing the harmless one-liners to fly under the radar but pulling them up on the more serious transgressions when the gags are off-colour.

One of our son's best foot-in-mouth moments came after watching Home Alone for the first time with his older sister. When my mother-in-law arrived at our place for dinner that Christmas Day, she turned to my son and lovingly proclaimed, "Merry Christmas, sweetheart!" My son instantly responded with a hearty, "Merry Christmas, ya filthy animal!" My mother-in-law's face just dropped with dismay. My husband, daughter, and I couldn't help chuckling because we knew where he got the line from. These sudden, inappropriate one-liners are a daily occurrence in our family, both invented and borrowed material.

Our teenage daughter also has a gift for saying inappropriate things, and we have had many laughs. She is creative, intelligent, and wise, but when those two little Gremlins – Ruby and Robert – come together, chaos often ensues. Our daughter's alters also cause a lot of laughter. For example, Genevieve – my six-year-old firecracker alter-child – is a constant source of family entertainment. There is never a dull moment when she comes out to play. With a broad American accent, she blusters and romps around, loudly demanding candy, toys, and Peppa Pig or Barbie on the TV, with the house in an uproar with all the commotion.

When my kids were younger, they were like the Gremlin twins with their creative trouble-making, which meant I needed to have eyes in the back of my head. Metaphor, sarcasm, irony and hyperbole can often be lost on ASD kids, who tend to take what is said quite literally. So, a common expression like 'Jump in the lake' to an autistic child can mean that you literally want them to jump in a lake. Late one afternoon, after our son had been a handful through the morning, I walked into the lounge room to see my daughter looking through a phone book:

"Mum? You know how you said that Robert was driving you crazy this morning? Well, I have a solution: how do you spell *orphanage?*"

"What?!" I said as I walked over to see what she was doing.

"Mum, I'm finding an orphanage to take Robert," she said as her little fingers flicked through the phone directory's pages. Barely restraining myself from uttering expletives in response, I was reminded that we parents of ASD children must also filter what we say, if for no other reason than to ensure the beans aren't spilled at the next family gathering … or to strangers.

I recall driving home from a restaurant on my husband's birthday with his mother in the car when Genevieve spotted a Vet's signage and suggested, "Mum, can we stop at the Vet's to get Robert spaded?" You should have seen my mother-in-law's face. Though I corrected her sternly, on the inside, I was laughing because I knew this was just another harmless example of the whacky things I hear daily in my parenting life.

A sense of humour is critical. Not only is laughing good for the mind and soul, but it is also a valuable coping mechanism for parents: a reminder not to take life too seriously; it's a 'reset button' of sorts. Raising my children has undoubtedly taught me this truth, and I am grateful. However, humour can only get you so far if a child's behaviour escalates to the point of a meltdown.

These days, I can often be heard saying, "I'm off to join the Circus", which indicates to my family and friends that I am having a bad day. By posting this comment on social media, my friends know to check in on me and offer some support and comfort. Having friends who are genuinely concerned to ask, "Are you okay?" and then listen to your subsequent download is extremely helpful and cathartic, sharing one's maddening burden before the ringmaster brings out the flying monkeys.

CHAPTER 7
I'M OFF TO JOIN THE CIRCUS

When I was a kid, I loved going to the circus. My parents owned a takeaway shop, and every year, Ashton's Circus would come rolling into town. They gave us free tickets for displaying their posters promoting the circus in our shop window. I remember the excitement of sitting under an oversized canvas tent filled with the smell of sawdust and popcorn. Excited cheers went up from the crowd gathered in the darkness as a spotlight lit up the ringmaster and the music played. The clowns would come rolling out in all different shapes and sizes. The acrobats juggled while the clowns provided comedy relief for the delighted audience.

From a young age, I could relate to the romantic idea of running away with the circus—leaving your worries behind and hitching your carriage to the rolling circus train as it leaves town for destinations unknown. Years ago, when I had a terrible parenting day, I thought I would let my friends know when things at home were not going well with the kids by simply declaring, "I'm off to join the circus!"

I wrote this chapter two years ago, tears streaming down my face, on one of those 'circus' days. I was up late, trying to organise the schoolwork for the following day since my children are schooled via Distance Education and are enrolled in a fantastic online school that supports students with disabilities. Our daughter was still up and couldn't sleep as she was having vivid hallucinations and was mentally unstable.

Her favourite coping technique during these psychotic episodes was to self-harm: to cut herself repeatedly. She battled severe suicidal depression, and her team of specialists worked hard to keep her alive. I eventually got to bed at 3 a.m. on this particular morning, thoroughly exhausted from lack of sleep and emotional distress, and I cried like a baby, angry that my daughter was suicidal again. I must expand on that statement: I wasn't angry at our daughter but furious at the pain she was experiencing; so much pain that it seemed to her that ending her life was the only solution.

I felt like we were trapped in a never-ending cycle that my child and I couldn't escape. A downward spiral of depression that kept going around and around relentlessly. But every parent – and it doesn't matter if your child is neurotypical or has a disability – will have 'circus' days. We all have emotionally draining days when we can hear a clown car beeping outside, bidding us to run away with all the other parents who are no doubt also escaping their seemingly insurmountable difficulties. However, our children depend on us to help them overcome such challenging times, so I want to share my strategies for overcoming a tough day in this chapter. I don't claim to know all the answers, but I know what has worked for me and what I feel is most important to share with you.

Mental Health Day For Parents

Parents, and especially mums, need the occasional Mental Health Day. When I feel overloaded and need a break, I will tell my hubby and kids I'm calling a mum's Mental Health Day. I ask them to keep the house calm and clean, to work together and most importantly, to be kind to mum. I am fortunate to have a hubby who helps with housework and child-minding on mental health days, and we buy takeaway food so that I can relax with a good novel and catch up on sleep.

I recently learnt that pain can be used as a powerful tool to drive through whatever life throws at us. Pain teaches us much about ourselves as human beings and as parents. My Mental Health Days are for when the pain of parenting becomes overwhelming, when I feel so emotionally overloaded that I can't bear it anymore – not one more problem – that's when I tell my family to "BACK OFF!" it's mummy's Mental Health Day.

The Joy Of Reading

Reading fiction books – novels and stories – is the best and most effective way to relax. Studies have found that reading fiction for 20 minutes daily has a soothing effect equivalent to an hour of yoga. A temporary escape from one's problems, reading fiction relieves the mind, regulates breathing, and lowers blood pressure. There are excellent public libraries nationwide in Australia with a fantastic selection of novels, DVDs, magazines, etc., and online resources such as e-books and audiobooks.

I worked in public libraries for eight years, and I know first-hand that there is no need to buy books or magazines when you can borrow them for free. You can buy used books, magazines, CDs and DVDs cheaply at thrift shops. Audiobooks are the way to go if you're not a big reader. I have listened to many books over the years, and this is an excellent way to relax and be entertained with fiction stories or learn something new by listening to non-fiction material while you clean your house or drive somewhere.

Medications and Supplements

I have found supplementing our diet with multivitamin capsules to be most beneficial. I take fish oil, Vitamin C, Executive B Stress formulations and Magnesium supplements daily. I have also been taking antidepressant medication for the past ten years. That is not necessarily a solution for everyone, but I found it tremendously beneficial in overcoming the worst of my PMDD condition, which featured monthly bouts of suicidal depression. Some doctors will prescribe medication for your child, but the decision to do so will be entirely up to you. You know what is best, but I was prepared to try anything to find something that worked. At some point, I realised that without this medication, I couldn't function properly as a mother and wife. Using antidepressants can be socially stigmatised, especially in Christian circles, but my husband is grateful that I am no longer a moody cow every month.

Journaling

Like reading, writing is proven to be good for the soul and is an excellent way of releasing all the negative emotions from the day. Buy an attractive journal and start writing down your thoughts and feelings at the end of every day. Alternatively, you can journal electronically; whichever you choose is entirely up to you, but writing down your reflections on life can cathartically release your frustrations. You can also retain your journals as lasting mementos you can revisit for years to come. Journal writing helps one reflect on good days and bad, record techniques for overcoming the bad, and offer the reassurance that good times will return when the storms of life pass.

My husband has kept an electronic journal for over seventeen years now. Of course, I am not allowed to read it because it is his way of processing life's challenges and recording the good times. I have to respect his wishes because I know that his journal is where he downloads his darkest thoughts. It is better left unspoken and unknown to me or anyone except God.

Find Online Connections For Emotional Support And Advice

The COVID-19 lockdowns reinforced the importance of the Internet for communication and demonstrated that we are still connected through networked technology, no matter how isolated or alone we may be geographically. Many of my kids' medical appointments have been conducted online, which is brilliant—especially for those living in rural locations like ours.

Over the years, I have joined many online disability support groups. At first, they were ASD support groups, but they have now branched into DID support and teen mental health and depression support groups. These groups are channels for reaching out worldwide and connecting with others who know what you are going through. We can share ideas, thoughts, and techniques for dealing with tricky situations. We can also make connections and build friendships over time, which can significantly benefit parents of special needs children.

Gardening

My garden is the window to my soul. I wanted to create a beautiful outdoor environment that my kids could enjoy, revelling in God's wonderful natural creation and enjoying a good daily dose of Vitamin D into the bargain. When my husband and I relocated to our tree change property eight years ago, I immediately worked on establishing a rose garden. I have over 30 bushes around the property and love nurturing my outdoor plant babies. The therapeutic benefits of gardening are well known, but like my husband, it's not for everyone. You may enjoy knitting, genealogy, sewing, painting or playing a musical instrument. Find something you are passionate about and give yourself a little time each day to focus on your creative endeavours.

Exercise

Regular physical exercise is essential for all, but doubly so when dealing with stress and depression. I'll be the first to admit to laziness concerning daily fitness routines. But I also know a healthy body equates to a healthy mind, so once again, find a physical activity you enjoy. It may be going to a gym, taking early morning walks or participating in some sport. I bought a cheap exercise bike and dumbbells that I use first thing in the morning, five times a week, whilst watching YouTube videos.

Contact Your Tribe

Call friends with special needs kids, those who know what you are going through and who understand what you are telling them. I offload on them as it is challenging to burden my husband with all my hardships constantly, and often, he is experiencing the same pain that I am feeling. As a mother, it is necessary to call on help and advice from 'your tribe.' You need a support group of like-minded parents in similar circumstances who genuinely understand what you're going through and are accepting and non-judgmental about what you share with them about yourself and your kids.

I am blessed to have a small tribe of amazing friends who support us through thick and thin. My best friends, Balfour, whom I have known since I was 15, and Ceils, the most fantastic parent of special needs kids I know, are two members of my tribe. Balfour encouraged me to write this book as I often downloaded the bizarre daily events of my life to him.

Ceils is my go-to person for advice. Full of knowledge and insight, she is like the Oracle from The Matrix films. She also has terrific special needs kids and is like a second mother to my daughter, whom she loves having stay-over as Ceil's daughter and mine are best friends. They have a fantastic time together, and I appreciate the respite when my daughter is away. Ceils is a perfect example of that friend with uncommon wisdom. She always knows the right words to say when I am very emotionally down or distressed. Ceils and her loving husband, Warren, are excellent parents; we are blessed to have them both in our lives.

I recall my first meeting Balfour with great fondness. I was 15 and dating one of his friends. Something about Balfour caught my attention: he understood my morbid sense of humour. I eventually broke up with his friend, but my friendship with Balfour blossomed into something resembling close siblings. We have been friends for over 35 years. Being one of three sisters, I have always wanted an older brother, and he fulfilled that role in my life. He was the first person I called when my husband had a brain tumour, and the prognosis was bleak. Balfour was at my wedding, and after telling my husband, he was the first person I called when I was diagnosed with melanoma. He has been my rock and remains one of my primary sounding boards.

Establishing a support network is crucial, even if it is only a handful of friends you can trust with your downloads. If I didn't have my team of friends to listen to me, I would feel lost and alone. They also share *their* battles with me, and helping others enables me to focus on something other than my own battles for a while.

The back of this book has a social media section where you can follow links to connect worldwide with other parents of special needs children today.

CHAPTER 8
TIME TO GET CRAZY – OUTSIDE-OF-THE-BOX PARENTING TIPS

Take On A Youthful Persona For Your Teenage Child

Okay, I will be the first person to admit I am a big kid – I always will be – but making my family laugh, especially when something serious happens, is my way of relieving the tension. I have an outside-of-the-box parenting strategies toolkit. When our daughter was 16, I began experimenting with a teenage girl persona called Geraldine to connect with my daughter on our movie nights. The idea behind this persona was to make myself more relatable to our daughter so she could connect with me emotionally and I could offer her advice as a friend. I look back fondly on those movie nights with popcorn, lollies, and laughter, like two giggling schoolgirls.

Using Hand Puppets To Open Communication Channels Between You And Your Child

When I spent time with my son, especially when he was younger, I adopted a wise-cracking, belligerent persona with a crocodile hand puppet. I applied a gentler, kind-hearted persona with his beloved childhood teddy at bedtime. He wasn't opening up to me about issues bothering him, so when I adopted these personas and animated his teddy or crocodile puppet, the communication barriers came crashing down. Although my son is now on the verge of becoming a teenager, these wonderful characters are still a significant part of his life today.

They say laughter is the best medicine, and it's so true! My dad taught me this truth by example, and I've passed it on to my children. My favourite alter-ego is Crocky, the green crocodile puppet. I explain that he is trans-species to my kids: "An alligator who identifies as a crocodile." I must say, I enjoy transforming into Crocky as there are no holds barred from what I can say. Yes, it is all PG-friendly for kids, but you can put a fuzzy green piece of material on your hand and listen to yourself transform into quite a daring and rude little cracker as you bring the puppet to life. I admire Jim Henson, the creator of the Sesame Street / Muppets characters, being enthralled with those shows as a child. Still, I believe that the one degree of separation puppets create makes them an excellent tool for working with children with special needs.

I use puppets to humorously and entertainingly educate our kids and advise them. This seems very practical, yet it wouldn't usually happen if it was just an old authoritarian parent-figure mum attempting to have a deep and meaningful conversation. Simply having your hand in a puppet causes children to open up emotionally and tell you what is on their minds. Affordable puppets can be found on eBay or Etsy.

Use Humour To Break The Ice

During one of her many 'bad days' when she was 17, our daughter and I happened to be talking about all the UFO reports in the news, but noticing her slashed arm, I quickly grabbed some oven foil and made a tin-foil hat and began wearing it. Perplexed, my daughter inquired why I had covered my head in foil, so I told her straight-faced that it was to prevent Alien Mind Control. In an instant, the mood in the room changed from melancholy to hysterical as my daughter's giggles echoed around the kitchen. It was an effective way of breaking the ice with my child. Robin Williams was one of my favourite actors. As a young university student, his movie Patch Adams impacted me and eventually influenced my parenting style. Letting go and being a child for a while can help your child deal with severe mental distress.

Hair Dye and Camouflage: A Superhero's Secret Weapon

As discussed earlier, experimenting with one's hair colour and clothing can empower autistic children and enable them to overcome their social awkwardness. This is because they can disguise or mask themselves and covertly walk the earth under the empowering cover of camouflage. The difference in their confidence when they step out of the house as their superhero alter-ego is astonishing. My children can have brightly coloured hair because they are homeschooled, but if your child is in mainstream school, school vacations or possibly weekends may be times when your own Wednesday or Pugsley Addams can shine. The impact will decrease as your child grows older, but the most important thing is that your child is outside of the house socialising instead of moping around the house or cooped up in their bedrooms with their faces pressed to a phone screen.

Halloween, Ministry Style!

This idea may be controversial to fellow Christian mums: participating in Halloween. Before I became Christian, I loved dressing up in spooky attire. My husband and I used to be immersed in the Goth subculture. The main reason I have allowed my kids to participate in Halloween is purely as a form of therapy. Hear me out: For kids on the Spectrum or who have severe anxiety, wearing a costume makes them feel comfortable going out and socialising with other children. Our rural area provides limited opportunities for social contact, so I encourage the kids to decorate the house and help with costumes. They can choose costumes that aren't scary or 'demonic', like angels, books, movies, or cartoon characters. This year, my son dressed as a Medieval Knight, and he looked great!

As for me, Halloween is an opportunity for ministry. What other time of the year do you get hundreds of strangers knocking on your door? I stock up on sealed lollies and attach a small Bible verse or tract to the packaging. I never say "Happy Halloween!" but "God Bless!" It's my way of taking advantage of a powerful opportunity to plant the seed of Salvation in Christ in the minds of these kids who door-knock my house every year. It also gives my kids a vital socialisation experience, allowing them to walk out the door in disguise once a year and fit in instead of being teased and ridiculed for being different.

I have a plethora of heartwarming, comedic tales to choose from. However, Autism and DID have a painful, dark side, such as severe anxiety to the point that my children have developed phobias. Obsessive-compulsive traits can have dramatic impacts on your child's life. My son is going through this. Losing one of his favourite therapists has caused some new, obsessive-compulsive behaviours that are somewhat concerning.

Living with Dissociative Identity Disorder (DID) brings a host of challenges, including chronic fatigue, flashbacks to past trauma, and severe anxiety and depression. There are days when our child struggles to even get out of bed due to overwhelming exhaustion and body aches. My heart breaks for her, especially after hearing my daughter say they wouldn't wish this disorder on their worst enemy. It's truly a brutal experience.

On the hardest days, I hold our child close and remind her that it's okay to feel upset. She needs to be free to cry, scream, and express her anger. Most importantly, Ruby must know I am here to support her unconditionally. Together, we will explore different paths and strategies to improve her quality of life. It's about finding the right "puzzle pieces" that fit, and I firmly believe that with time and persistence, the complete picture will emerge.

CHAPTER 9
EXPECT THE UNEXPECTED

I have previously discussed some wild and woolly days when I felt like a pioneering adventurer, venturing into unexplored territory and not knowing what to expect. Most days started calm and collected, but by day's end, there was often a raging inferno in my living room that had to be extinguished.

I had the most beautiful brindle-mottled Persian-cross cat, Ursula, who became Ruby's companion in her early years. Our daughter was an only child for a long time, fully seven years old before she had a brother, so Ursula was an important early childhood friend to her. When we first brought our baby girl home from the hospital, Ursula was intrigued and tried to figure out what the baby was. She smelt my scent on our daughter and soon became fiercely protective of the baby, like Nanny Dog in Peter Pan. She kept guard through the night, sleeping on our daughter's nursery floor. When our daughter cried, she would trot down the hallway and into my bedroom to wake me up with a gentle whack to my face to alert me that something was amiss with the baby.

One day, our daughter played with green slime and put the gooey mixture on Ursula's fur. I was furious because removing the slime from the cat's fur was difficult. So, as I cut the hardening slime-matted clumps of fur from the cat, I thought about how I could get through to Ruby. I wanted to teach her a lesson because she felt what she did to Ursula was funny. Encouraged by having some leftover goo remover in the cupboard, I devised a scheme to make her aware of the consequences of her actions, and so I gently took a handful of slime and mixed it into our daughter's hair. In an instant, her laughter turned to tears. "Now, Ruby!" I triumphantly told her, "What's good for the goose is good for the gander." She sobbed as I asked, "Will you ever put anything in Ursula's fur again?"
"No, Mum," came the reply. I took her to the bathroom, applied goo remover, and washed her hair. She never put anything in the cat's fur again, fully understanding there were consequences for doing so.

Ursula's "I am not impressed" expression, sums up Ruby's childhood antics nicely. In this instance, she's nonplussed with the party hat Ruby has furnished her with.

For this reason, sometimes you have to do the same thing to your children as they've done to others so that they understand the consequences of their actions. You need to read the situation and ensure this approach is safe for the child. Because I had orange oil, I knew I could easily remove the goo without cutting Ruby's hair.

That didn't stop Ruby from applying my favourite, limited edition Avon lipstick all over Ursula's face to turn her into the

Joker from the Batman movies. A month after the sliming incident, I heard our little girl singing in the bedroom, and I smiled smugly, thinking she sounded like an innocent angel. I shuffled down the hallway and casually looked in my room only to be confronted with Ursula, staring back at me with a distressed "HELP ME!" expression on her lipstick-smeared face! All this poor cat – 18 years old by this stage – could offer as she looked up at me was a pathetically weak "Meow." So I grabbed my ruined lipstick, which to be honest, had to be thrown out as I found lipstick plastered around my cat's bottom. Our daughter was banned from using her iPad for a week after I ineffectually attempted to clean the oil-based lipstick out of Ursula's fur with baby wipes.

One Sunday about two years ago, when our daughter was already 17, there happened to be a baptism at our church. When we walked into the church and took our seats, everything seemed normal enough: Ruby was herself, and all was well at first. But upon seeing the baptismal font, our daughter's six-year-old alter Genevieve, presented like Rick Mayall's imaginary character in *Drop Dead Fred,* mischievously declared loudly, "Look,

Mummy! – a swimming pool! I want to go swimming." Knowing she would readily jump into the font if she could, I immediately restrained our daughter and asked my husband to help me escort her outside so she wouldn't disrupt proceedings. In some situations, the only thing we can do is to quietly remove our children from triggering environments. This is a perfect example of a circus day: if a clown car had pulled up, I would've jumped in without hesitation and driven off into the sunset.

Another weird and wonderful experience with Genevieve was when we stopped at a roadside takeaway on a busy highway to order burgers and hot chips (fries) for dinner. Again, Ruby was around 17 at the time, and on this day, she said she felt 'dissociated,' which is to say she felt a little unstable and on edge. When I hear Ruby utter that word, I know it is likely one of her alters will present themselves. Hubby ordered our meal and waited inside the shop whilst I remained in the car with Robert and Ruby. We were discussing our plans for the weekend when a large truck filled with chickens in cages pulled up behind us.

It was apparent the poor birds were heading to a chicken processing plant. The truck driver got out, a plump man in his late 40s wearing a singlet and jeans, wiped the sweat off his brow and entered the takeaway shop. It was a hot summer's day in Australia, in the mid-30s Celsius (around 95° Fahrenheit). Now, the chickens in the cages became restless and began squawking, with their vehicle being stationary on a hot day and no cooling wind circulating around them as it did when they were underway. Without warning, the words, "Hey, smelly, where are we?" emanated from the backseat of the car in a familiar, throaty tone. Genevieve was with us! "Smelly" is Genevieve's nickname for Robert.

I instinctively locked all the car doors – thank God for central locking – as I didn't want her to leave the car and run onto a busy road, chasing my daughter. But she could hear the chickens and turned to look out the window to see what the commotion was all about. Seeing the poor chickens and realising their grim fate, great distress ran across her face, and she became determined to get out of the car and free the chickens! Imagine 300 loose chickens scattered across a busy road: it would look like a real-life game of Crossy Roads, only with roadkill everywhere. "Hey! Let me out, Mum! I wanna free the chickens," she demanded, as she kept working the door handle to try opening it. Thankfully, my knight in shining armour arrived with dinner just in the nick of time, and we made our speedy getaway into the sunset without causing major traffic altercations between cars and chickens.

One of my treasured moments with Genevieve was Mother's Day, a few months after the chicken incident. I asked Genevieve to come out on this special day and do my make-up because she'd been asking me to do my make-up for the longest time. I have photos of our daughter smearing makeup all over my face – making me look like a clown – much like she did the cat when she was little. I laughed so hard as she concentrated and earnestly declared, "Beautiful! Beautiful!" repeatedly in her gurgling childish voice whilst haphazardly applying the mess. Looking at the results in the mirror, I resembled a Goth after a hard night of partying, with blotchy, deep purple eye-shadow and bright red lipstick smeared across my face … I have a soft spot for this little one: I get to time-travel and revisit my daughter when she was a sweet and innocent child.

I particularly enjoyed it when Genevieve did Ruby's makeup when she was about to go out. On another occasion, Genevieve was out and decided to give herself/Ruby a well-deserved makeover. I could hear Genevieve singing a Taylor Swift song in a sweet six-year-old girl's voice, so I was curious and went to the main bathroom. I popped in to see Genevieve/Ruby's face arrayed in brightly glistening colours, resembling an amateur drag queen ready to take the stage. "Beautiful, sweetheart!" I exclaimed, and Genevieve smiled contently at my comment. I held back from laughing and excused myself to return to the kitchen to finish preparing lunch.

Ten minutes later, a piercing scream shot through the house, and our daughter came running into the kitchen, mad as a cut snake: "Mum! Look what Genevieve did to my face; she's done my make-up!" she said furiously. I chuckled, saying, "I know. I went into the bathroom ten minutes ago and saw her beautiful creation." Ruby busied herself with make-up removal wipes and scrubbed her face to remove all evidence of the makeover fiasco. "Now you know why God created make-up remover wipes," I declared, giving her a warm hug. When alters (or parts) take control, the primary identity will be unconscious. They don't remember anything that happens at these times. This is caused by the previously mentioned amnesia wall, which separates the parts of the personality into individual identities.

My strategy with the alters is to treat them like distinct individuals, different to our daughter, because that is exactly how they present. At such times, our child is not Ruby per se but Genevieve or Edmund, so I must apply parenting techniques to a six-year-old girl, a nine-year-old boy, or even an adult. I treat the alters like they're my children, too, and ensure they feel welcomed and loved when they present. Parents of DID kids should accept these alters as they each have a particular role in helping their child. The frequency with which our daughter's alters appear is decreasing as Ruby gets older and works through her deep-seated issues in therapy.

When our daughter was first diagnosed with DID, I didn't understand that I needed to recognise the alters for special occasions such as Christmas and Easter. This was all new to me. I wasn't aware that each alter must have its Christmas present under the tree. This was an important lesson, and I now make sure that my alter children have a surprise under the tree each year.

The Case Of The Killer Pyjamas. It was two in the morning, and my son, who was nine at the time, was running a high fever. I was up with him and went to the kitchen to get some medicine when my daughter walked into his room and, talking in a gruff voice reminiscent of Neil from *The Young Ones,* said hoarsely, "Hey, mum! My pyjama pants are trying to kill me!" Our son immediately stopped crying and broke into a big grin, thoroughly amused.
"What?!" we both asked simultaneously, trying to confirm that we heard her correctly.
"My pyjama pants are trying to kill me! They're moving slowly toward me on my bedroom floor." My son and I both burst into incredulous laughter. We weren't making fun of her, but the

bizarreness of her claim just set us off. My son was sick, I was sleep-deprived, and my daughter dropped this bombshell about killer pyjamas. It was a left-of-field statement: obviously, my daughter was having a psychotic episode and hallucinating – both symptomatic of Dissociative Identity Disorder – so what to do?

My strategy in such circumstances is to calm my child down with food and drink. Eating or drinking stops psychotic episodes dead in their tracks because the familiar motions and sensations involved in the physicality of drinking and eating are psychologically grounding. Hot chocolate and something to chew and swallow were in order. The episode subsided within a few minutes of eating, and she was back to normal.

When my daughter was first diagnosed, I felt overwhelmed, but then I did some research on the internet and read posts from other parents in similar circumstances. I was interested in how they dealt with these strange situations. Sadly, I found precious little in the way of personal stories and advice about parenting strategies that worked for parents of these children, but rather a lot of high-brow, technical, and medical information with only a few practical suggestions.

Another strange incident occurred about six months after the killer pyjamas incident. At dawn one morning, I heard an odd sound from the lounge room: "Time for Teletubbies! Time for Teletubbies!" I got up quickly, knowing something weird was happening, and opened my bedroom door to see the entire contents of my fruit bowl arrayed neatly on the floor in a perfect line leading to the lounge room. It was like the Hansel and Gretel fairy tale with their trail of breadcrumbs.

Sure enough, my daughter Genevieve was in the lounge room watching *Teletubbies*. To my surprise, our gorgeous son – only nine years old at the time – was on the couch opposite, keeping an eye on his sister. My son told me Genevieve woke him up at 5 a.m., but he didn't want her to disturb my sleep, so he got up and cared for her. My heart melted: what a sweetheart! In this instance, I told Genevieve firmly that it was too early and that she should go back to sleep.

"No!" she responded abruptly, in a defiant *Drop Dead Fred* voice. So, I stayed with her while my son returned to bed. We watched two Barbie movies before Ruby returned, dazed and confused as to why she was on the couch at dawn, watching Barbie movies. I filled her in on what had just happened, and sleepy and emotionally spent, she returned to her bed, and I could also head off and get some much-needed rest.

Another of my daughter's beloved alters is skate-punk Edmund. A young man of about 23, he has spiked-coloured hair and face piercings. He also loves to ride his skateboard. His personality is reminiscent of Tim Curry's character, Frankfurter, from The Rocky Horror Picture Show. He is unique, very quick with one-line comeback responses, and has a wicked sense of humour. I fondly remember Edmund's antics at one of our son's birthday parties. This was Robert's first birthday party at our country home. Balloons filled the room, kids were madly running around in the lounge room, and I was in the kitchen preparing party food. Ruby was in the office working on the computer when one of the children, a little boy, came into the room and started hitting her on the head, repeatedly asking, "Does this hurt?" each time. Ruby was handling it very well and thought it was entertaining.

Suddenly, Ruby froze like a statue, and I knew she was switching to another alter. I could see the entire interaction from the kitchen. I saw her facial expressions change to sneers, and I knew Edmund was present. He turned to the child who was still hitting him on the head and responded, "You're an annoying little cracker, aren't you?" He then looked up at me and whispered, "Help." I quickly entered the computer room and ushered the child back to the main room.

Edmund was relieved and said, "Thanks, mum. I woke up, and a strange child was balloon bashing me on the head." I smirked and said, "Edmund, it is a children's party for Robert. Want to come to the lounge room and join in?" He responded, "Hell No! I'm escaping the madness. But you can bring me food. Do you have any Skittles?" Skittles are Edward's favourite lollies (candy), and I always have a bag hidden, especially for him. I brought him the bag, and his face lit up. "You're awesome, mum. Now, shut the door. I have gaming to do." I kissed him on the forehead and closed the door.

I returned to the kitchen and finished the food preparation for the party, thinking how remarkable it was to have different children living in one body. Every special needs kid is different. Our kids have different health diagnoses, so different household rules and routines apply to each of them. They are each unique and unforgettable because they dance to different tunes. They take their unusual circumstances and learn how to make it all work for them. I admire this adaptability greatly. We can learn a lot from our children regarding resilience and how to successfully overcome life's challenges.

My experiences with parenting our alter children have taught me a valuable lesson. There's still only one way to love, so be flexible and adapt your environment to your beautiful children's needs. I like to say, "Embrace the insanity!" My husband and I have been doing this for years, although it has taken him a little longer to accept that my daughter has a mental health condition. But once you have had a few strange encounters, you gain familiarity with it and parent accordingly. Just like Gremlins, there is a simple rule. No, it isn't "Don't feed them after midnight." It is this: *Call your child by their alter's name when they're present.* That's it! Calling your child by their birth name and not their alter name causes severe anxiety and unrest as it is disrespectful to your child and the alter. It increases trust issues and puts up a barrier between you and your child. No matter how they present, you should always try to show them love and reassurance.

Our son also has his moments of mischievousness. The kids were still little when we first moved into our country home. Our son was about four, and our daughter was eleven; her alters were still dormant at this time. I had finished homeschooling the kids on a rainy day, and my two little monsters went outside and started chanting, "We are children of the mud!" in a hypnotic cycle. I was preparing for the next day's lessons on my computer but stopped to listen. It reminded me of a scene from *Lord of the Flies*. I got up and took a peek outside my kitchen window. The kids had mud stripes on their faces, like soldiers in

Vietnam hiding from the enemy. They were circling around and relentlessly chanting their slogan.

Okay, that's creative, I thought, so I sat back at my computer and continued working ... until several big thuds could be heard slapping against a window. I stormed onto the back patio and saw they had thrown mud against the sliding door I had just come through. I was about to get angry with them and then started laughing when I realised that the kids were mistakenly throwing dog poo instead of mud. You should have seen the panic on their faces when I pointed that out to them. I hurried them inside for a scorching hot, super soapy shower, then went out and hosed their 'creative work' down before it could dry.

After cleaning up the mess, I was very agitated, but I sat down to work at my computer again when I heard liquid splashing onto our tiled floor. I got up to discover my son had found a four-litre (one-gallon) bottle of vegetable oil in the kitchen pantry and poured all the contents onto the hallway floor. I screamed "NO!" in horror, but as soon as I did that, our overweight staffy cross, whose excrement the kids were earlier throwing onto the house, ran up the hallway in excitement and slipped on the oil, hurtling herself into the bedroom door at the end of the corridor. The poor dog looked like an out-of-control seal, legs in the air and flailing helplessly on her back. And the mournful yelping noise she made when she hit the door haunts me still. The kids lost their iPads for a few days over that one, but I spent an hour cleaning up the oil with a bucket of water, vinegar, and dishwasher liquid. If you ever need to remove cooking oil from tiles, a lot of vinegar does the job efficiently.

Now that our kids are much older – 19 and 12 – the frequency and intensity of their mischievous Gremlin-like behaviour has reduced dramatically. Our daughter's alters don't present themselves nearly as often as they used to, except Genevieve, who makes a grand appearance every couple of months or so when my daughter experiences a significant triggering event, or more likely on special children's occasions like Christmas Day and birthdays. Being with Genevieve is strangely soothing and therapeutic, like turning back the clock and spending time with my daughter when she was still a child. Genevieve doesn't age and still loves playing with dolls, watching Barbie movies, and deliberately calling her brother "Smelly" to upset him. You can hear her voice echoing around the house when she comes out, loudly and excitedly announcing, "Mum?! I'M OUT!!" When she comes out late at night, it can be pretty startling, to the point where I have come close to falling out of bed.

From my years of parenting our DID child, I have noticed that there could be a correlation between imaginary friends and DID. Before the alters made themselves known and our child began switching identities, our daughter talked about having imaginary friends. From the research I have done, imaginary friends in childhood is a common experience for people with DID, and this is a strong indicator that the rare condition is present. It is not a definitive marker, but an interesting correlation exists.

Our son is the apple of my eye, and parenting this child is a pure joy now that he is older. He has the most fantastic sense of humour. The incident with the slide operator, telling him about how good my 'bum and boobs' were, was a little clue that his extraordinary personality would grow in time. Like his sister, he went through puberty early, but because of these startling changes, he became my Siamese twin: we're joined at the hip.

What makes my son so unique to me is his ability to take a stressful situation, usually involving his sister, and find the humour in it to turn it into an occasion for laughter and stress release. For example, he shoots hoops in our courtyard, he plays guitar, and when the subject of band names came up, he suggested 'Dawn Of The Dorks.' Now, that's pretty creative. Robert also has a caring nature and is a beautiful young man I am so proud of. Like most other boys his age, he loves computer gaming, but he also has a talent for visual arts and creates the most impressive sculptures using modelling clay, as mentioned in an earlier chapter. I encourage any creativity, especially with the hands, as hobbies and interests like this develop a child's fine motor skills, and autistic kids need to work harder on those skills.

One last example of our son's fantastic humour happened a few years ago when he was having his fortnightly session with an occupational therapist. She was teaching him about appropriate and inappropriate touching and personal boundaries. Our son asked her if it was okay to touch chicken breasts. She burst into laughter, and he smiled cheekily. All his therapists love working with him because of his beautiful, gentle nature and wonderful sense of humour. That night, I asked him to take the chicken breasts out of the fridge so I could cook a stir-fry. He replied, "Mum, are you sure I can touch the chicken's breasts? I haven't gotten permission …" I turned to take in his wonderful smile, his eyes mischievously lit up, and I responded with a grin, "Don't be a smarty pants. Get me the chicken's boobies!" to which he roared with laughter.

From these personal stories, I hope you can see how a good sense of humour is alive and well in our household and how it is used to de-escalate and cope with stressful situations. Parents of special needs children need to nurture and foster a light-hearted and humorous disposition. This is a very effective tool for overcoming adversity.

From personal reflection, I have had days when the bizarre events were so strange that I needed to process them to ensure I interpreted them correctly. Then there are days when I don't want to get out of bed because I feel so overwhelmed and mentally exhausted. I find that the theme song of the animated TV series Ruby Gloom sums up my family nicely:

S-so today, we're gonna;

Take the time to show ya;

The br-br-bright side of the dark side;

Br-br-br-bright side of the dark side ...

– Ruby Gloom theme song.

Your sense of humour can help you relieve mental stress through the power of laughter and joy. For example, my husband came close to death from a brain tumour when our daughter was only four months old. His headache lasted for days, and then the pain intensified quickly. Thankfully, when his mother took him to the hospital, he projectile vomited on arrival, which caused him to be promptly attended to. I received a phone call later that evening asking me to come and say goodbye to my husband. He was on death's doorstep because he had a litre of fluid in his brain cavity: a cancerous brain tumour blocked the flow of liquid from his brain into his spine, and that mounting pressure was killing him. The doctors didn't know why he was still alive as he should have passed away with his brain under so much pressure within his skull.

Surgeons arrived that Sunday night to perform an emergency procedure to drain the brain fluid. Surviving that procedure, he would have another eight-hour brain surgery two days later to remove the tumour. My husband didn't want to go into surgery without seeing me first. He has an incredibly dark sense of humour, very Monty Pythonesque. I smiled and kissed him warmly and told him how much I loved him and that he would get through this.

Just before the orderlies hurriedly wheeled him through the doors to the operating theatre, I whispered in his ear, "You know, the positive thing to come out of this is we now have proof that you have a brain." His face, filled with trepidation, suddenly lightened, and he smiled wryly. He was still smiling and waving as the orderlies whisked him away. What was my motivation for doing this? Well, I wanted my husband to go into the surgery smiling instead of fearing the worst. I also knew that this warped sense of humour is our love language, and if God was going to take him that fateful night, at least he'd go out smiling and relaxed. God performed some miracles with that whole drama, and the doctors couldn't understand why he was still alive and talking coherently when he arrived, and then the surgery went well.

He had a litre of fluid drained from his skull and had the tumour removed days later. Never underestimate the power of prayer. The use of humour in this instance is an example of an out-of-the-box strategy that I usually apply to our kids. As the saying goes, *When life gives you lemons, make lemonade!* My husband teases me when I use this phrase and comments, "You know you are saying that our kids are lemons." My response to this statement is, "You know I am talking about making something good come out of a stressful situation." My parenting approach is an example of how you can handle a highly stressful and frightening life-changing situation with humour and dignity, but most importantly, with the power of prayer!

CHAPTER 10
TIME TO FORGIVE YOURSELVES AND OTHERS

There is a strong temptation to self-blame when you realise your child has a disability. As a mother, you might begin by reflecting on your pregnancy: did I eat the right foods? Did I take all the necessary supplements? Is there something I could have done to prevent this disability from manifesting in my child? Blaming yourself is natural, but it is also irrational. No matter how much you shame yourself, it won't improve your child's situation. You will never know the cause of your child's health issues, but what you need to do is accept their diagnosis and move forward.

When our autistic daughter received a second diagnosis (Dissociative Identity Disorder), I started to blame myself even though it was caused by a childhood trauma that my husband and I weren't even aware of until many years after it happened. When we were informed of this trauma, we talked about whether there were any signs we had overlooked.

When she was seven, my daughter would mysteriously say, "There are things you don't even know about me, mum." When I tried to press her on that comment, she would slam shut as tight as a clamshell. When the amnesia walls my daughter had built to protect herself came down many years later and we found out what caused the trauma, I was so angry! I wanted to lash out, smash things, scream and yell. And then I grieved our child's pain.

I realised that I needed to forgive myself for not being aware of what had happened and forgive those bullies who caused my child's pain. If I kept hold of the anger, it would've turned to bitterness, and I'd be allowing them to keep hurting us and not be able to parent at my best, with the clear thinking and rationality I needed to help our children. So, after a few months of processing the revelation, I began looking at ways to heal our child and myself.

After my husband's brain tumour, things were rough in our relationship, and so we underwent marriage counselling with a Christian psychologist at a local church. We faced many issues, and it was about six months after my daughter was born. Gary, the psychologist, told us about Epictetus, a Greek Philosopher who is famous for saying, **"It's not what happens to you but how you react to it that matters."** (MLA. Epictetus. *The Golden Sayings Of Epictetus.* Champaign, Ill.: Project Gutenberg, 1997). Epictetus's worldview resonated with me. I embraced this view and reinforced this idea with our kids.

Another lesson God taught me was that having a sounding board other than your partner is necessary. Your partner is also hurting, so it is most beneficial to confide in someone outside of the family whom you trust, who can bring some objectivity in helping you to analyse your situation. When our daughter was first diagnosed with DID, I did plenty of research on the condition to have informed conversations with a few close friends with whom I confided to get their advice on what they would do in my situation. Our daughter is on a journey of grief, reflection, processing, healing and moving forward.

Forgiving those who harmed you is a way of regaining control over your life. I still wish to jump into Doctor Who's Tardis and rectify the situation, but that dream is entirely unrealistic. There is currently a lot of doom and gloom in this world, so it is essential to stop and smell the roses. To get through each day, we must remember that no matter how bleak things get, tomorrow is a new day, full of the promise of better things and positive experiences. Forgiving yourself for your parenting mistakes and forgiving those who have hurt you is the first step to moving forward. When we do this, we are letting go of the past and building a bright future for our family.

We don't teach kids the act of forgiveness nowadays. The most important lesson we, as parents, can pass down to our special needs children is to show them how to take control of their lives. Forgiveness is a slow and convoluted process, but when achieved, you and your child can move forward without being hobbled by the awkward baggage of past wrongs. Our children's mental health is at stake, so this is important. Forgiveness is the door that loosens the grip on your child that their tormentors have over them. However, forgiveness is one of the most challenging attributes to develop. I have witnessed a lot of bad behaviour by kids over the years, and I've seen their parents shift the blame or deny that anything ever happened. Parents are not teaching their children to be accountable for their bad behaviour.

Self-forgiveness is also needed for your past mistakes before you became a mum. We often think back to when we were younger and the stupid things we may have done: the wrong boys we dated, the off-colour things we might have said to people we loved. Do you know what I am talking about? Regrets and missed opportunities: 'what-ifs.' What if I didn't do this or that? Wouldn't I be so much better off now? Those what-ifs are a normal part of our inner lives as we work to interpret and understand the pain we experienced when we were younger that we haven't fully processed and released. It is like having a lead ball chained to your ankle, slowing you down and preventing you from arriving at your final destination.

I devised a technique to stop ruminating on negative memories from the past and on those people who have hurt me. I visualise a cemetery in my mind and mark the gravestones with specific bad memories or the names and faces of people in my life that were no good for me. Whenever I reflect on a painful memory, I visualise taking it to that old cemetery in my mind, complete with wrought iron gates, withered trees and crumbling gravestones lit by a full moon, and visualise engravings on those tombstones with the names of people who have hurt me in the past. As I visualise a person's name or specific event on the headstone, I say to myself: *What is in the past stays in the past.* Doing so stops me from reliving that painful memory, and I can instantly be fully present in real time, focusing on what needs to be done. Eventually, those ugly memories fade and lose their power over me. This unusual approach has worked for me, and I am currently doing it less often.

Prayer is vital for forgiveness as I take my problems to the foot of the Cross. We offload our spiritual burdens but also learn to build a relationship with God by trusting Him to heal us and our children from past mistakes and wrongs that have been done to us. All this takes time and repeated effort. God is fantastic at building patience in people, and I should know. I used to be very impatient, but the continual washing of the Holy Spirit has eroded my impatience and replaced it with strength and tenacity. Pray every day over an issue and eventually, when the time is right, God will help you let go of the past and focus on a more positive, productive future.

A word of caution, though: forgiveness doesn't mean trusting someone who has repeatedly demonstrated their disregard for you. Everyone deserves a second chance, but to readily again trust someone who has betrayed or abused you is foolish. The narcissists we encounter in life will always seek to take advantage of us because they are completely self-absorbed, self-righteous crybullies. The best advice for your safety and protection is to distance yourself from such people. Christians, in particular, are easy prey for narcissists since Jesus asks us to be loving and treat others as we would like to be treated. But He also warned us to be as wise as serpents, so we should be wary of people who try to take advantage of our generosity of spirit.

CHAPTER 11
SAYING SORRY

I could be a better person. Our kids know this when I make a mistake or say something I regret. I sit them down and apologise for my bad behaviour as soon as I cool off. My kids didn't come with an instruction manual. I sometimes wish they did, but I apologise to them when I behave poorly and have a distressed mother's meltdown spray. I want them to know that parents aren't perfect, but when I am wrong, I will admit it and ask for their forgiveness.

Being honest and admitting when we are at fault is essential to parenting. Not only will your children respect your honesty, but they will also learn that to err is human, and they can apply the valuable principle of repentance in the many instances when they make mistakes, whether at work or in their personal lives; that it is dignifying to say sorry and face the music. I have met many parents whose 'perfect' kids can't seem to do a thing wrong. Still, they're spoiling their children rotten and instilling a sense of entitlement that breeds arrogance, brittleness and irresponsibility in adulthood.

There are a lot of Christian mums who should know better but will unquestioningly defend their children's bad behaviour. I have seen Christian parents witness their kids' lousy behaviour, look on in silence and disregard it. Sadly, this self-righteous, hyper-protective attitude persists even in country church circles, where our children have been bullied. Most of our moves to different churches have been in search of congregations that live out the love of Christ, which includes the love of truth and correction with their parenting: to be humble and teachable.

By not teaching children accountability, they are setting their children up for a world of hurt when they grow up. It only takes one ill-conceived statement or wrongly perceived word for an alcohol-fuelled, self-righteous hot-head to king hit someone and drop them to the pavement, causing them brain damage or even death. You are doing your child a disservice by not addressing this bad behaviour now before they reach adulthood.

I admire Ceils as a mother for encouraging her children to understand what they have done wrong when they make a mistake. In the early days of our friendship, our same-aged daughters didn't get along well at first. We were all at another child's birthday party when this beautiful woman with long, golden-brown curls and big blue eyes introduced herself and immediately apologised for her daughter's bad behaviour, explaining that she had punished her for mistreating my daughter. You could have knocked me over with a feather! I have never had another parent apologise for their child's behaviour. I knew from that instant that this woman was exceptional, and I immediately wanted to befriend her, and I did! Our daughters became best friends, and Ceils proved to be the strongest, wisest and most resilient mum I have ever met. I look up to her as she's honest and forthright – telling it how it is – and the kindness she has shown my kids over the years has brought tears to my eyes.

It takes guts to apologise to a stranger for your child's culpability in an incident. Still, by admitting that your child has done wrong, setting a suitable punishment and apologising to the child's parents, you teach your child life-long skills in dealing with adversity. Adopting the principle of honest admission – of saying you're sorry – instead of mounting a blind defence of your child grounded on the false assumption that they can do no wrong will make you and your children better people.

I am the first to admit that our kids aren't perfect; sometimes, they can be little rotters. But when they have done wrong, they are held accountable. Having special needs children is difficult, but don't confuse a disability with your child's bad behaviour. Kids will exploit your weaknesses as a parent and use the disability card to get away with unacceptable behaviour. Both my kids have done this, but after a while, you get a feel for ASD-related behaviour and actual bad behaviour.

Once your child has been diagnosed, carefully monitor what sets them off. It could be a TV ad, loud noises in the house, or even the light bulbs irritating your child's eyes if they are photosensitive. Through observation, trial and error, determine what sensory issues your child might have and the resulting behaviour, then make corresponding changes to their environment to see if you can minimise those irritations and improve their emotional regulation. It may be as simple as adjusting the TV's sound volume or changing the light bulbs in your house to a different type of bulb, colour, or brightness. There are answers.

CHAPTER 12
GETTING ORGANISED

The role of therapists, support workers, and other medical professionals is to help your child thrive and have a fulfilling and successful life. Being organised is challenging, but my husband has slowly helped me improve, as this is his area of expertise. Some women are so organised that their pantry shelves are proudly featured in lifestyle magazines. Everything in their bedroom closet is neatly arranged, folded, labelled, boxed, hung and stacked.

Unfortunately, I have trouble in this area. If you open my clothes drawers, you will see a mess of clothes tightly squashed into those small spaces. The drawers don't close properly for all the overhanging items, and I struggle to find time to store seasonal clothes. Similarly, my office desktop is littered with clutter collecting around my computer. I have amassed innumerable pieces of paper, notes scribbled on them and pushed to the back and bottom of my desk drawers. By contrast, my husband's key skills include decluttering and organisation: his clothes are neatly folded in the drawers of his dresser, and his computer workstation is clean and uncluttered. We are like Oscar and Felix from the TV sitcom *The Odd Couple*. I am like Oscar, the messy, fun-loving and careless slob, while my husband is like Felix, the well-organised partner who prompts me when I leave a spoon on the countertop or neglect to refill the toilet paper holder. We are opposites in this regard, but I admire his organisational skills.

Hubby has a degree in Information Management, and it shows. He does the budgeting and calendar scheduling to ensure we know when the bills must be paid and what happens on any given day. He diligently tracks our scheduled appointments, meetings, events and timetables in our electronic calendar, which we call 'the brain.' Social events, anniversaries, special occasions and holidays; medical appointments, school class times and supporting specialists' visits (such as tutors and occupational therapists) as well as our kids' outings with support workers are all included in the brain, informing us of when and where something is happening or when we need to be somewhere.

Once the regular, repeating weekly, monthly and annual events were entered into our common-platform electronic calendar – in our case, Apple's Calendar app – the simple rule is to add an appointment to the brain as soon as it is made. Ideally, we open the brain before calling to make an appointment so we can enter it right away and avoid clashes with other appointments. We know very well that if we leave entering the date for later, we can easily forget to do it at all. That can create chaos when we receive an unexpected knock on the door or the dreaded "Where are you?" phone call from an offended party. This happened quite a few times until the disappointments of missing out and hubby's lectures reinforced the importance of this family being conscientious with keeping 'the brain' fed and current.

That small initial effort has a significant effect. Yet, even though our daughter has access to the brain on her phone and computer, she can be pretty neglectful when adding her appointments to our calendar. We consequently went through a time when we were often surprised by the unexpected early morning arrival of a support worker at our front door, ready to work with our daughter while she was still asleep and I was in my pyjamas.

Life is much easier when 'the brain' is kept up-to-date and working correctly.

I also keep a written list of the most critical appointments in a small notebook because I don't carry mobile electronic devices with me everywhere. This is my preferred option for tracking what is happening day by day. Like their paper equivalents, electronic calendars and scheduling apps allow mums to track and plan their days and remain organised easily. At least two behaviour specialists who have worked with our children have stressed the importance of visual daily planners.

Our daughter was too old and independent-minded to submit to keeping a schedule when we first attempted to introduce one. She tore down all the visual planners we hung up in her room and study area, so we kept the scheduling to ourselves and applied it to her life to create some structure, if not routine, in her daily life. As I started earlier, our son was much easier to work with, and he was homeschooled from the outset. We are still working to teach him the importance of routine by ensuring he completes something every day, but our daughter, who also has ADHD, is still having problems getting organised. Indeed, she is one of the most disorganised people I know, but she is young, and the demands of modern living will teach her over time.

Implementing routine in the lives of ASD children is known to be a compelling technique for helping them structure their otherwise chaotic lives. Our hyper-sensitive ASD kids' anxiety is exacerbated by uncertainty: not knowing what is happening and when. Change is unsettling for them, and when life is chaotic and unstructured, their experience will seem like an endless stream of upsetting changes and surprises. This is why your ASD child wants to know what's happening first thing in the morning, and frequently asks about what's happening next throughout the day.

From personal experience, I have snapped at my kids for forgetting to tell us about a specialist meeting or a support worker coming on a different day. Hence, a visual planner is great for all family members to know what needs to be done or where we need to be for an appointment at a given time. The younger the child learns to work to a schedule, the easier and less stressful your life will be. You will also be helping them develop organisational skills that will reduce their anxiety, increase their positive self-image, and enable them to achieve great things in life.

ASD health professionals have also encouraged us to implement a reward system for our children. Our successful system involved large jars and little cotton balls or pom-poms. A cotton ball is added to the jar for each chore or good behaviour your child performs or demonstrates. When the jar is full, the child is given a reward: it might be a small toy, experience or monetary payment big enough to motivate them to keep going and refill the jar for their next reward. The choice of reward is up to you and can be negotiated with your children if you desire, but the point is to motivate them to do their chores, teach them to value working to improve their circumstances and gain some power. Our children have outgrown the rewards jar, but like the daily routine planner, the younger you introduce this system, the easier it will be to get your children involved and actively participate in keeping the household tidy, clean, and pleasant.

For many years, I lived on reduced hours of sleep because of my eldest child's health issues. I am very blessed to be able to catch up on sleep later in the day because my hubby works from home. If you're a single or working mum and have no other carers at home, that's impossible, so I recommend establishing set sleep routines and not staying up longer with your kids, even during holiday periods. Whenever I stayed up later with my kids, it would not be easy to reclaim and revert to my usual sleep time the following evening. I learned early on that my kids perfectly exemplify the adage, *Give them an inch, and they'll take a mile.*

Safe, homeopathic and herbal sleep supplements are available to help your child sleep if they need it, but please always consult your doctor first. To help our daughter fall asleep when she was younger, we often left her with audiobooks to listen to in bed. We typically ran Audio CDs borrowed from our public library, although nowadays, many electronic audiobooks are available from library eResource pages. But from the variety of stories our daughter heard, she gained a remarkable grasp of English, and the stories cultivated her fertile imagination. If your child has difficulty going to bed or falling asleep, they might be interested in listening to audiobooks on their favourite topics.

My organisational skills are best exemplified in how I perform my household chores, and these ideas can be helpful to others. Before I go to bed, I pack the dishwasher to run in the morning, as we have solar panels, and I try to minimise electricity usage at night. I also pack the washing machine and have it ready to run the next day. In summer, I run the washing machine late in the afternoon and hang the washing out in the evening to avoid the sun because of my fair skin and vulnerability to skin cancer. I also cook large batches of food for our main meals, so there will be ample leftovers for reheating the next day, reducing my weekly cooking time. I will also freeze surplus food in containers for reheating on those lazy days when I want a break from cooking or on those hectic days when I can't seem to find the time to cook. It's cheaper and more wholesome than buying takeaway food.

Because I homeschool, I leave the bigger household jobs such as carpet cleaning or defrosting the freezer for the school holidays.

I record when these jobs are done for reference, so I know when they're due again. I always have drinking straws handy for icy cold drinks to help with meltdowns, as the sensation of drinking something cold through a straw calms our kids down. I also have frozen juice ice blocks ready because the cold sensation distracts and de-escalates their panic attacks and tantrums.

Medical professionals such as occupational therapists, psychologists, and allied support workers are at the heart of the operation, pumping the lifeblood of wisdom and professional care through the family body. Believe it or not, having a support worker take your child on excursions out of the house is necessary. Why? Because your child can become emotionally dependent on you if they're around you all the time, and that isn't good for their development. So, encouraging their independence by providing opportunities to explore the world and learn new skills away from home, such as engaging in various outdoor activities, sports or hobbies, benefits both of you as you can appreciate a much-needed break to relax or catch up on housework.

I have seen much positive growth in my children's personalities since support workers started working with them. But how do you choose which medical professionals and support workers to become involved in your family support network?

CHAPTER 13
SELECTING THE RIGHT PIECES TO YOUR PUZZLE

It is overwhelming when you finally get the news that your child has a disability. I know from experience because I held my breath for a second but then realised I finally had an explanation for my children's unusual behaviour. When a Children's Autism Clinic was assessing my daughter for ASD, I asked if they could also test my son. When one child in a family has autism, your other children will likely also be autistic.

Once the diagnoses for both children came through, I knew that I needed a planned approach to addressing my children's needs. The National Disability Insurance Scheme (NDIS) had just been implemented in Australia, so I knew I had funding. Still, I wasn't allocated a support coordinator: a disability specialist who could suggest practical ways to help my children in terms of accurately assessing their functioning capacity and suggesting pathways and health providers to help them. I had to figure out what was needed, so I researched extensively. Once the kids were asleep in the evenings, I would spend hours reading autism specialists' recommendations on effective forms of therapy, and I discovered the main categories of professional help for autistic children are occupational therapists, speech pathologists, psychologists, psychiatrists, support workers, and behavioural specialists.

We worked with the same psychologist intermittently for five years until she retired when the pandemic started. I decided to give my son a break from psychology appointments but kept that form of support going with our daughter. She was with another psychologist for a couple of years until we found her current psychologist, who specialises in trauma and DID. It takes a while to know if the selected form of therapy, or even a specific individual therapist, can help your child. If you find a given health worker is not helping your child, find someone else and keep changing them until you find someone who is a good match and is helpful. The same is true of the various forms of therapy; some will be more effective than others.

After moving to the country and undergoing more rounds of trial and error testing, I finally found my daughter's current and primary support worker. Apart from taking my daughter to medical appointments, weekly therapy in the city and assisting her in dealings with government bureaucracy, this outstanding individual has been fantastic for my daughter's mental health and has gone above and beyond in both providing support and keeping me informed about my daughter's concerns. She has a way of encouraging my daughter to try new things and overcome phobias, such as entering large shopping centres. She has saved my daughter's life on numerous occasions by supporting her during bouts of suicidal depression. She has a beautiful heart and is a gifted support worker with a background in psychology and a passion for working with people with disabilities. She has gone above and beyond in helping our family, and I can't imagine where we'd be without her.

She has taught our daughter many life skills, including cooking, personal safety and applying social skills in public. I shed tears of joy when that support worker sent photos of themselves standing in the front row of my daughter's first adults-only rock concert. This was a significant achievement as my daughter had an agoraphobic condition for some time, where she wouldn't even take so much as a step out of our house, to where she was now attending rock concerts alongside thousands of people. My daughter can be pretty unstable – fine one minute and severely distraught the next – but with the help of her mindful assistant, she remained calm and enjoyed herself.

We had another fantastic support worker whom I endearingly call 'Poppalicious' as I considered her a real-life Mary Poppins. Sadly, she moved away, but whilst working with my kids, they both adored her with her brightly coloured hair and clothes and infectious positivity. Life was highly entertaining when she was around, and I looked forward to seeing her fly in, just as curious to see what brightly coloured, jazzy ensemble she was wearing on the day. A highly energetic and adventurous young lady, she was great for taking our kids on outdoor activities like hiking through forest trails, swimming in rivers or beaches, and even canoeing at a nearby lake. Outings with her were just as much fun for our son as for our music- and art-loving daughter, with whom she attended rock concerts and frequented arty shops and cafe walks.

We now have six different support workers for our kids, and they all provide a fantastic array of services to help our children. At times, our home is as busy as a train station, with everyone coming and going. Having a common family calendar – the brain – has been essential to tracking when support workers are coming to take our kids out and when they'll be back. Support workers also give us some downtime. I even owe my ability to write this book to the fabulous brother and sister team Nick and Billie-Jo, who run the disability support agency we have settled on, again after much trial and error. These professional problem-solvers have years of experience and know our children's entitlements and needs regarding health services. They understand how the system works and where to look for the missing pieces in our children's disability care puzzle, and they know how to implement these helps. They are also kind and passionate about working with people with disabilities. What more could you ask for? We are blessed to have them involved in our children's daily care.

With parents of special needs children, it is often the little things that make a big difference, like when a non-verbal autistic child verbalises a sentence for the first time or when a child achieves anything that doctors said would be impossible for them. Little miracles will happen daily if you have faith and pay attention to the details. Outside-of-the-box thinking is your gateway to exploring new or alternative therapeutic approaches such as naturopathy, equine therapy, art therapy, music therapy, and gaming therapy, which are improving the lives of autistic kids. Trial and error applies here as well. All you can do is select a treatment you or your child are interested in and try it. If it doesn't work, try something different. Your child's medical treatment is like a jigsaw puzzle. You try a piece, and if it doesn't fit, you remove it and try another until you find the right piece.

CHAPTER 14
RESCUE THERAPY

Introducing pets into your family life during your children's early years is a compelling form of therapy. Not only do pets provide constant companionship for your children, but pets also have a way of connecting with kids and helping with their disabilities by intervening, distracting and appeasing them, enabling them to regulate their emotions. I find rescue animals from shelters, especially older ones who are no longer babies and have much love to give. We purchased a fantastic dog, Lola, eight years ago. She has changed our family's life forever and was an immediate answer to prayer immediately.

We had just bought our house in the country and promised our daughter that she could have a dog as soon as we were no longer renting, which was in itself an answer to prayer. Our daughter asked God for our own house so she could have a dog. Once we settled into our home, I began investigating charities that re-homed rescued dogs. I registered with about six charities and hadn't heard anything for a long time. I wanted a sterilised female dog that was at least a year old and that was good with kids with disabilities and cats (because we already had a rescued cat). That's a pretty tall order. We heard nothing from the online charities, but one was of particular interest to me – Pound Rescue, based in Sydney, who were focused on rescuing dogs that were on the 'kill list' at dog pounds around New South Wales and Queensland. I remember the night they contacted us very clearly: my daughter was whining impatiently about how she would never get a dog. I told her to leave it up to God, assuring her that He would give her the perfect dog, and I topped off my lecture with the old 'patience is a virtue' chestnut. My husband suggested we pray, and so we did, together as a family.

Now, I am not kidding about the timing: not five minutes after we prayed, the phone rang, and it was a lady from Sydney whom I had never met or conversed with, but she told me how she had a special dog for us and thought we might be suitable candidates for her 'forever home.' We believe that a pet is a pet for life – a family member – and we do not turn from our commitment once we bring a pet home. The unique dog in question was rescued from a dog pound in Northern Queensland, where the charity had just spent $3,000 on curing her from a severe case of parvovirus.

The lady was anxious to affirm that we earnestly intended to keep her 'forever' and wouldn't be sending her back, and she assured us that the dog was excellent with cats. I was so excited, and with a big, beaming smile, I said we would take her without a prior inspection. The Australian 'tyranny of distance' was very much in play. I put the phone down and informed the family that God had answered our prayers. I was shocked as I had never seen such an excellent, rapid response to prayer.

A week later, this beautiful, tan staffy/ridgeback cross with pretty black 'eyeliner' around her eyes like some ancient Egyptian princess was delivered to our doorstep. The first thing she did when we let her loose in our house was run down the hallway and jump directly onto our daughter's bed with a massive grin, eyes beaming, and her tail wagging excitedly. She had found her forever home, and our daughter couldn't have been more delighted.

Lola has been a fantastic addition to our family, especially concerning our now ageing cat Rachel, otherwise known as Darth Kitty. Our brindle rescued cat has angel feet and one tooth. She had a gum disease and lost all her teeth except one by the time she was three years old. Rachel runs the show, and I find it funny to hear Lola whimpering at night because she is trapped in the bathroom (where she goes to eat the cats' food). Rachel sits in the bathroom doorway and won't let Lola out. If Lola is overexcited and scampers around the house, Rachel will swipe her on the nose to settle her down. Though Lola is a 30-kilo ball of muscle and could easily crush Rachel, she takes the swipes with little more than a squeal or bark. When a neighbour's cat once jumped into our yard to beat up Rachel, Lola swooped outside and aggressively chased the other cat out of our yard.

Three years ago, we added two more felines to our home. Brother and sister Morty and Gigi help with our kid's anxiety and depression with their entertaining antics. They get along quite well with Rachel and Lola, but Naughty Morty, the caramel crop-circle patterned cat, always gets into mischief. At midnight one evening, while my husband and I were watching a movie in our bedroom, we were startled by a loud noise like a gunshot at the opposite end of the house. Oddly, the kids didn't wake up, but we rushed out to find our beautiful, big (6 x 3 foot), ornately-framed hallway entrance mirror in a shattered mess on the tiled hallway floor. We suspected Morty had jumped on top of the mirror, which was sitting on top of our hallway table, chasing a moth near the ceiling and brought the whole lot crashing down, smashing the vases, picture frames, and potted plants that were in front of the mirror; broken glass, pottery and soil everywhere. We were livid – the mirror was part of my husband's deceased aunt's estate – but the awkward clean-up would have to wait until morning not to wake the kids.

I call our home 'The Menagerie' because we have one dog, three cats, and two guinea pigs. Two special needs kids and numerous visitors complete the picture. My husband and I are the wardens who run the show – or try to! Our guinea pigs have provided much joy and cuddles over the years. A guinea pig is an excellent, low-cost pet if you live in a confined space, like an apartment. They need a daily cuddle and a weekly wash and dry outside in the sunshine whilst you clean out their cage and lay new straw bedding. Hamsters, mice, fish, and pet birds are fantastic additions to an ASD family but the bigger, furry creatures are more fun. Pets teach kids responsibility, patience, kindness, and how to connect with a living being emotionally. Because autism is a neurological disorder that impedes ordinary communication, ASD kids can have difficulty making emotional connections with people, but having pets from a young age will help develop those nurturing and empathetic qualities in your child's personality.

The death of a pet is brutal for any child, but especially for ASD children, and yet this too, is an important life lesson. When my 18-year-old cat Ursula passed away, my daughter, who was seven at the time, was devastated. She was so upset that she couldn't calm down. So the next day, we returned to the pound and adopted Rachel, the rescue cat. We cared deeply about Ursula, but our daughter was on the verge of throwing up from the distress she felt, so we believed we could skip a lengthy mourning period.

Rachel got our attention by tapping hubby on the head from her perch as we walked through the enclosures at the pound, trying to pick the right cat for our daughter. Our daughter approved, we brought Rachel home, and my daughter was smiling again. Although she still missed her lifelong but elderly furry companion who sat by her crib in her infancy, she was excited to have her very own cat and not share her mother's cat, which I had adopted many years prior when I was still at university.

All animals have a sixth sense when something is wrong. When I had panic attacks in my early 20s, Ursula would sit beside me, tap my face and gently nip my arm to calm me down and coax me out of the episode. Our kids have confirmed the same. When my daughter was in a bad mental state years ago, the dog and the three cats scratched and head-butted her bedroom door. They wouldn't stop. On one occasion, it was two in the morning, and I had just gone to bed thinking my daughter was asleep. But thanks to our furry friends, their ruckus at her bedroom door saved her life as I investigated to see what all the commotion was about. This is why having your child bond with pets from a young age is essential. Even if your child is not on the spectrum or doesn't have a disability, pets provide extra protection by being your child's constant companion. If you are a pet-less family with kids with disabilities, please consider adopting a pet.

CHAPTER 15
NEW EXPERIENCES

ASD kids don't like change. Change can be positive or negative, but we can't stop change, so we must teach our kids from a young age that although change might be scary, it is necessary for their growth. Theme parks are great places for children to be challenged, overcome and grow.

My son recently went to a water park with his support worker, and on a specific raft ride, the passengers had to sit around the vessel to balance the weight distribution. The assistant in charge of the ride directed my son to sit in a spot between strangers, away from his support worker. This was quite an awkward and uncomfortable request for my son, and when he attempted to return beside his support worker, he was told to sit back down at the spot allocated to him. He complied and had a wonderful time going down the fast water rapids. Being in a confined space and then pressured into compliance could have induced a meltdown, but he chose to 'suck it up' and remain in his designated spot, for which he was amply rewarded.

We all know that 'patience is a virtue', and parents with autistic kids also know patience is in short supply with their children. Just the simple act of queuing can teach our ASD children the gift of patience. All theme parks have long queues for rides, sometimes up to an hour or more for the most popular rides, but this is a fantastic opportunity for our children to learn about the rewards that come with patience and perseverance.

Another significant attribute of theme parks is that they encourage a sense of achievement by overcoming one's inhibitions and fears. Some kids are scared to go on a particular ride because of the speed or noise that it makes. Encouraging your child to try something new, unfamiliar or frightening is a lesson in perseverance, overcoming hardship, and self-imposed limitations. Your child may avoid going on a given ride, but each time you go back to the theme park, you can keep encouraging them to try something new, and they will eventually overcome their fears and anxiety and jump on that ride. This is when we praise them for their bravery and determination.

I always wanted to go to a rodeo, so we seized the chance when a bull-riding carnival came to a nearby town. The spectacular bull-riding was supported by loud music, pyrotechnics and motocross stunt riders performing mid-air somersaults. It was like a rock concert with an extravagantly theatrical stage show. We took our son to this spectacle to reward him for how hard he worked during the school term and because hubby and I are so proud of the fantastic young man he has become. It was a lovely, kid-friendly, family event, and we chose to sit close to the action with our folding chairs rather than in the grandstand further back.

Unfortunately, our spot was close to the speakers, which taxed our son's noise sensitivity. We hadn't anticipated that the event would be so loud, so we didn't bring noise-cancelling headphones or earplugs. However, I created some makeshift noise pads by folding some stacked facial tissues and placing them over his ears, the pads held in place by his hoodie. At first, our son pushed his fingers into his ears, but my improvised noise cancellers worked wonderfully, and he could sit back and enjoy the show. I always bring our children's favourite snack foods on our outings, just in case things get hairy. Eating can prevent a meltdown from occurring or reduce the severity of panic attacks.

A heart-stopping incident happened that night as I wore a black and white Frisian cow-print cowboy hat and a matching black and white jumper. A particularly aggressive, sizeable black bull was on the rampage, looking for another victim after forcefully bucking the rider off his back. As the bull restlessly paced the gated rodeo ring, head-butting the fence to look for an escape, he came to where we were sitting and stopped for a few seconds, staring into my eyes. My heart rate quickened alarmingly as the bull snorted and looked fixed to charge at me, but then the rodeo workers caught his attention and corralled him into his enclosure.

Immediately after this incredible, heart-stopping moment, my son whispered, "Hey, mum, I think the bull fancies you because you look like a Jersey cow." I looked down at my black-and-white jumper and realised he was right! A few hours later, he asked me what I would have done if the bull had managed to break through the gate to get to us. I replied, "I would've shoved the black and white cowboy hat on dad's head, grabbed your hand and ran off in the opposite direction." He roared with laughter, and I also learnt a valuable lesson: never wear clothing that could have you mistaken for a cow at a rodeo. Our son thanked us for the best day ever: the randy bull at the rodeo topping off a fun day at the water park with his favourite support worker. His happiness warmed my heart, as our son was often starved of attention while we concentrated our parenting efforts on our more troubled eldest child. So, having one-on-one time with him will be locked in my memory forever.

New experiences are essential for ASD kids. Attending music festivals and standing in the front row of a crowd of thousands, conquering the theme park ride that initially scared them witless – overcoming fear is always a significant achievement. My son eventually went on rides he was so scared of at the water park that he wouldn't even venture near them. Over the years, I have seen my children grow in leaps and bounds. My children couldn't go into a takeaway shop and order a meal, let alone spend time in a shopping centre, because of their hypersensitivity to the bright and flashing lights and the general rumble of conversation between people in those crowded spaces. My children have adapted to previously uncomfortable environments and grown emotionally and socially because of their support workers' enthusiasm for working with children on the spectrum. In Australia, we are fortunate to have excellent government support for anyone with disabilities, whether children or adults, but without loyal and dedicated support workers, many people would be left behind.

Familiarity with parents tends to breed complacency, where support workers invigorate and encourage our children to try new activities that develop life skills, resilience, flexibility and adaptability to change. When choosing a support worker, ask friends and parents in similar circumstances to your own for recommendations. Personal references are the quickest and best way to find the most capable and effective support workers. If you don't have many friends using disability support, contact a disability support network for advice and recommendations. You can also find recommendations posted on social media support groups.

CHAPTER 16
FORMING CONNECTIONS

Dating

For the longest time, the subject of dating filled me with dread. We have a beautiful, intelligent daughter who had adolescent boys wanting to take advantage of her.

There are warning signs of impropriety on a date, and I am too forgiving, with my tendency to assume I am overreacting when my suspicions are aroused. So, I encourage you to trust your instincts. Dating is a complicated business even for neurotypical individuals, but for young people on the Spectrum, it is a treacherous minefield. The modern advent of online dating complicates the situation even more because of the dependency on trusting the other party to provide accurate information about themselves that cannot be assessed against the body language messages we receive in face-to-face interactions. Gone are the golden days that I grew up in, when one might meet a boy at a Friday-night disco, have a quick kiss and be home in time to watch MTV music videos with one's friends. The Internet has revolutionised how people form connections, their manicured profiles propped up beside a virtual highway that anyone can access – hence the danger!

We didn't allow our daughter to open a social media account until she was 16. However, I didn't expect sharks to be lurking so close to shore. In less than 24 hours, our daughter was targeted by a manipulative scoundrel based in a third-world country who pestered her for inappropriate photos. I am so glad common sense prevailed, and she didn't do anything stupid. But online predators lull young people into a false sense of security by complimenting them and building trust; then BAM!! – they attack!

My advice is that it doesn't matter how old your ASD child is; they are at risk of being taken advantage of and need supervision and surveillance, especially when in their early teens. Because ASD is a communication disorder, they have difficulty discerning deception and deceitfulness, especially when reading messages because the clues aren't as obvious. Hence, the Internet exposes them to manipulation and bullying.

ASD girls are trusting, admirable, and virtuous, but those qualities can also land them in a world of hurt. I will never forget how manipulative and hurtful my first boyfriend was, but I believed his lies … up to a point. He has since been twice divorced and has a gaggle of children to different wives, so I owe his first wife a huge debt of gratitude for taking the reprobate away from me.

I have a close relationship with our children, but I have concentrated primarily on our daughter and helped her through potentially catastrophic dilemmas over the past few years. She knows she can tell me anything, but there were warning signs with some of the boys she dated that she hid from me. I could have intervened earlier if she had shown me some of their phone messages. One kid had 'potential teen killer' stamped all over his forehead from my eventual reading of his abusive phone messages. Still, our daughter hid those messages and only showed me the kind and loving stuff, so I had no clue what was happening.

As happened with my first boyfriend, another girl became involved with this ne'er-do-well, which proved to be a marvellous and significant blessing for us: an answer to our prayers for protection for our daughter. That boy's new partner was also mentally unstable and aggressive, so the two deserved each other. Yes, our daughter went through a terrible time of mourning over her first love and recovering from the heartbreak, but she has since met the most fantastic boy, whom I treat like my son. One door closes; another opens. I have often found that grand new vistas will open when a door closes on those falsehoods we have been precious or dogmatic about. If you care to notice, people will show you who they are, so here are some warning signs that the individual your daughter is dating may not have honourable intentions.

Warning sign 1: If your daughter's partner won't come to your home and meet her parents and the rest of her family, they are likely hiding something. As a parent, you should force the issue and demand an audience with your child's new flame. Investigate immediately, as this is a big red flag.

Warning sign 2: The new partner frequently cancels dates with your daughter. When planned dates and meetings are commonly cancelled with flimsy excuses. This is a sign that they are playing the game, have hooked another victim, and are reeling them in. They'll say, "I don't have time to see you!" I have told our daughter repeatedly, "If a boy cares for you, he'll make the time; he'll move heaven and earth to be with you."

Warning sign 3: Highly problematic family life. It's a welcome sign that your child's partner respects and cooperates with their parents, but if their parents infantilise them, that parent-child dynamic is screwed-up. Your daughter will never be entirely accepted by a son still clinging to his overbearing mother's apron strings, nor will your son obtain the respect of a girl who has learned emotional manipulation from her controlling mother. Please help your child escape such relationships before they get too serious. I had our daughter join me in binge-watching a season of a reality show about women marrying men who haven't cut the umbilical cord, and that woke her up to the consequences of dating such men.

Warning sign 4: Self-absorbed individuals who are obsessed with their appearance and cannot share a mirror. Good hygiene is essential, but a chronic obsession with appearance and clothing can be a warning sign that Kissing Point Road ends at Dumpsville. Boys and girls who are obsessed with superficial appearances are life-sucking vampires. They only care about themselves, and you can protect your child from another discarded, empty husk left in their wake as they move on to their next victim.

Warning sign 5: They're super-stingy and expect your child to pay for everything. Yes, times are tough or exceptional circumstances may arise, but if your daughter is often paying their way through dates, she is likely being manipulated. There is no excuse for a young man to have no money to spend on his date constantly. If he's jobless or not given any pocket money, he can get welfare or a part-time job: his parents will appreciate their son working for an income. However menial the job may be.

Warning sign 6: Shoplifting. Petty thievery is another tell-tale sign indicating a flawed character, whether out of desperation or for cheap thrills. I have friends who have discussed this issue regarding their child dating a shoplifter. As far as I am concerned, making the excuse that big businesses won't miss the stolen goods reveals that the boy's heart is in the wrong place.

Warning sign 7: Cruelty to animals. Though my daughter's first boyfriend wasn't given to this heartless practice, *my* first boyfriend was. He would treat pets terribly, and on one occasion, I was alarmed that he was excited that a car hit a cat in front of us. The animal was still alive, so he was pleased to put it out of its misery. Sadistic torture and killing are very different to hunting and killing for food; it's one of the signs common to all serial killers. They are deliberately hardening their hearts to feel nothing for their victims. I should have heeded the alarm bells and ran quickly and far away. As I have said before, I was very naive and trusting as a teenager, but I grew older and wiser.

Warning sign 8: No practising faith in the partner can be a significant issue, especially for Christians. While there are kind non-believers, a partner who believes there is no God presents challenges in a relationship built on Christian values. The Biblical command "Do not be unequally yoked" is emphasised for good reason: being a faithful Christian means being in communion with Jesus and aligning with a Biblical worldview. Believing and honouring God is vital. Without faith, the spectre of meaningless suffering and hopelessness looms large, increasing vulnerability to suicidal ideation. Moreover, if a child has been raised in a Christian environment, they will likely develop a sacred respect for human life. It's also noteworthy that young Christians who marry non-Christians often find themselves drifting away from their faith. Ultimately, it is not your decision who your child should marry or whether their partner shares their Christian beliefs. All you can do is support your child to the best of your ability.

Warning sign 9: Personal influences, including social media and music, offer valuable insights into individuals. People's choices about what they watch and who they follow on social media reveal much about their values and interests. Modern teens often gravitate toward prominent YouTubers who definitely embody the term "influencer." Reflecting on this, it's essential to remember that you, too, were once a teenager trying to find your tribe. However, social media feels like a foreign concept to me, perhaps because I view it as a time-consuming distraction. To better understand this landscape, I sought advice from experts.

I wouldn't say I am fond of mobile phones: I consider them a necessary evil. Until recently, I primarily borrowed my husband's phone when I was out somewhere. Interestingly, he keeps his mobile phone switched off most of the time. While some people feel they must always be reachable, that's not the case for us. When I was growing up in the '80s, telephones came with long cords that allowed us to drag them into our bedrooms for lengthy, secretive chats with friends. Since the advent of mobile phones in the early '90s, communication has transformed dramatically. Nowadays, many teens find it challenging to engage in in-person conversations.

As a parent, reviewing your child's new partner's social media accounts can provide valuable insights into their personality. By observing their likes, dislikes, and what they choose to post about themselves and others, you can better understand their character and assess whether they might be suitable partners.

Warning sign 10: Your child's state of mind and physical well-being. Keep an eye out for a change in your child's personality and whether there are bruises or marks on your child's body. Monitor your child's mental state as the relationship grows. If you see dramatic improvement, that is a good sign. If your child starts to withdraw from you and their friends, this indicates there could be trouble, and you should investigate.

A word on bullying: euphemistically referred to as 'negative friendships' by some of our daughter's teachers when she was in the public school system. Both my kids have experienced such negative friendships: what a farcical term! Let's call it what it is: *bullying*. Whether in a crowded urban schoolyard or isolated in a rural church playground, it is difficult for autistic kids to meet others with whom they can form good friendships and who will respect them and value their company.

Like ASD girls, the boys are also overly trusting. Our son has only a handful of friends, most of whom are online. He has a few in our street and at church, but we homeschool online because we live in a rural area, and our local schools have a well-known reputation for bullying autistic kids. Unlike some parents, I do believe autistic kids should have their own specialised classes away from neurotypical children for their own protection, as well as for individualised, nurturing attention from teachers. ASD kids are often brilliant geniuses in their field of interest who need a more advanced curriculum in their area of gifting. Yet, they can display behavioural problems when subjected to noisy or bright environments and can be easily distracted by social pressures. This is my own personal opinion from my teaching experiences years before I had children. I applaud mums who send their special needs kids to public schools, but we decided this wouldn't be the best option for us.

If your child is being bullied at school, take photos of any bruises or wounds, keep a diary, and continually complain to the principal. If nothing is done, take it further to the Department of Education. If these matters are not resolved and your child's mental health is deteriorating, I would suggest you withdraw them from regular school and enrol them in an online distance education program to protect them from harm.

Believe it or not, there are amazing online schools that include face-to-face classes with teachers via computer technology. The kids can exchange email details and develop friendships. Many of these children are victims of serious bullying and have left the public education system for that reason. From personal experience, the online school we use has an excellent Curriculum and covers stimulating topics during the term. For example, my son just studied about the important role of Gladiators in Ancient Rome. For a 12-year-old boy, this was a fascinating subject to cover.

With the help of therapists, ASD kids can become resilient and learn ways to handle everyday social situations, but it takes time in a safe environment. Because of technology and social media, the dangers of bullying are now occurring in our homes without us being aware. If your child is being bullied to the point of severe anxiety and depression, please seek urgent medical help immediately and look for alternative schooling solutions. Please don't wait for them to become suicidal or violent. Your child's life could be at risk!

CHAPTER 17
GROWING UP

I started writing this book – my dream project – two years ago, but family dramas put my book writing on hiatus for an extended period. In hindsight, it was good to have a break from writing because now that our kids are two years older, our home dynamics have changed a lot, and for the better.

Our son is 12 and in his first year of high school. He's grown to six feet and inherited his father's gorgeous corkscrew hair. He now has a deep voice that adds an extra comical dimension to his frequently outrageous utterances. He's witty and outspoken but has a heart of gold. When I'm feeling down, he's my happy thought.

Our daughter is 19 and has grown into a beautiful young woman with an individualistic style that draws envy from other teenagers. She is becoming entirely independent and is focused on her chosen career path. This is what I wanted for our rainbow baby, a term commonly used for the first child born after a miscarriage. It is gratifying as a parent to see your once-lost child making her way out of a dark and foreboding forest into a flowery meadow bathed in sunshine.

I wouldn't say I enjoyed growing up, and I much preferred childhood. I found the physical and emotional changes that came with puberty most alarming: the distress compounded by bullying and rejection from my peers. Our son feels the same way that I did at this stage of life, and so I can relate to his exasperation and anxiety. He quite plainly states that he wants to remain a child and doesn't like the changes he's going through, but my husband's genes ensured an early puberty. Towering above other boys his age, he nevertheless retains a childish fascination for Lego: his significant, assembled kits cluttering our once spacious house. But this hobby is fantastic for improving concentration and developing his fine motor skills, perseverance and problem-solving ability. His horizons are opening up as his boyish fascination with cars grows into a full-blown aesthetic, shared with boys and men the world over, and he longs for the day he graduates from riding bicycles and scooters to driving cars. It seems growing up has its benefits after all.

Unfortunately, our daughter has emotionally distanced herself from her Christian peers because of the betrayal and mistreatment she received from other children at church and even from adult professing Christians. We keep reminding her not to let Christians get in the way of Jesus and that He was killed by 'religious' people. We encourage her to focus on Jesus because it is only in Him that we can genuinely say our best days are ahead of us.

Because we are an 'alternative' or an unusual Christian family that resembles the Addams family in many ways, another pearl of wisdom I share with my kids is that Jesus was, in fact, the counter-cultural, alternative person who ran against the grain of normative religious practice in ancient Israel. He hung out with people who were considered the dregs of society: tax collectors and prostitutes. But Jesus was looking at their hearts and not their external appearance, which is a mere shell that is shaped and buffeted by this sinful world. In the UK and the US, alternative churches have been formed by punk rockers and Goths who have entered into full-time Christian ministry. They have set up churches for people who embrace alternative music and fashion subcultures. Their services are filled with people with tattoos, coloured hair, and body piercings but who are on fire for God. This is how a church should be: welcoming and focused on people's souls rather than on their fashion sense.

As I matured, I became less interested in nightclubbing and refocused more on live concerts by '80s bands touring Australia. My husband recently bought me a gorgeous handmade wooden cross from Armenia, and when I wear it, I'm reminded of how much God has changed and shaped me. As my kids get older and more independent, I feel that I am 'finding myself' again. I'm not as consumed with parenting as I was, and my personality – other than being a mother – that has been dormant for so long is coming out now that family life is much calmer. I enjoy increasingly frequent and lengthening periods of downtime, where things are going smoothly in the household, and I can reflect on how we survived and got here. I think hubby and I have matured like fine wine, being able to see the results of

God's intervention in our lives. We are far from perfect but increasingly conforming to Jesus' image.

Have we been criticised by other Christians for not conforming to their cookie-cutter image of what a Christian should look like? Oh, yeah! We have faced much criticism from many church-going people who are extraordinarily self-righteous, legalistic or arrogant. Still, we can't look into their hearts to know if they are genuine Christians or wolves in sheep's clothing. Only Jesus knows the state of their heart, but if these people would start practising what they preach, many more believers would be seated in church pews on Sunday mornings.

I have seen severely intellectually disabled people attending a church and the church members complaining that they were too noisy! This snobbery is exasperating, but some Christians are set in their ways and may fear those who are different. Yet in the Bible, we read that God performed many miracles, so surely He can open our eyes to realise that people with disabilities need our love and support, not shooing away as if they were pests. God sees our hearts, so let non-Christians see what God has done for us by being known as people who love those who are different, unconventional thinkers, or, most importantly, those with disabilities.

CHAPTER 18
THE UNKNOWN

The spiritual realm can be a divisive topic, and as a Christian, I understand I will likely face ridicule for discussing it. However, it's crucial for me to address this subject. I have left it until the end because it has been a significant issue for me, especially since our kids were born. I'll say it plainly: it is well-known that individuals on the spectrum perceive spirits. The Bible states, "the dead know nothing," and refers to those who die in Christ as being 'asleep,' awaiting resurrection into glorified bodies suitable for eternity. It also mentions angels and demons, as well as evil spirits. The essence of this discussion is that children with Autism Spectrum Disorder are witnessing something from the spiritual realm.

I have spent hours on the Internet researching this topic, and I came across many articles and personal accounts from parents who affirm that autistic kids are particularly susceptible to experiencing supernatural encounters. Why? Because their brains are wired differently from neurotypical kids.

When my daughter was only one year old and still a baby sleeping in her cot, I heard singing over the baby monitor in her bedroom. But when I went to investigate, the singing stopped, and no one was there. And yet, when I returned to my bedroom, the singing would start again. This was before surveillance cameras were cheap and readily available. I had no idea what it was: static interference perhaps, or stray radio waves being picked up by another mother's baby monitor who lived close by. Maybe I was tuning in to a neighbouring mother singing to her own child. I tried changing the channels on my baby monitor, but the singing continued.

This singing only happened twice, and I eventually forgot about it. Still, when my daughter was about five, we were having breakfast at the kitchen counter one morning when she put down her spoon and asked, "Mummy, is my mummy from Heaven going to sing to me tonight? I miss her." I went pale as those strange singing episodes came flooding back to mind. It was real, and my daughter remembered this even though she was so young.

This was the first of many supernatural experiences in my house. My kids saw 'shadow people' outside our car, on the side of the road, while we were driving along a highway at night. My daughter complained about seeing someone on the side of the road covered in blood, trying to wave our car down to stop, but there was no one there. After a few of these episodes, I considered the many unexplained supernatural experiences I had as a child and decided to do some online research. I found many blogs and forums where parents of ASD children shared their experiences and discussed the same issues around strange, inexplicable sights and sounds.

From those forums, I discovered that the worst thing you can tell your child after seeing something strange is that it's their imagination playing tricks on them because it isn't. As Christians, the Bible teaches us extensively about what is unseen and how dark forces exist. What your child is seeing is not their imagination – it's real – and if you make fun of your child and reject their claims, it will cause them to withdraw and no longer confide in you. Their anxiety levels will dramatically rise because the problem they've raised remains unresolved, and these unusual incidences will consequently increase in frequency and intensity.

When you shut your child down and negatively dismiss their observations as mere imaginary fantasies, you sever the line of communication between yourself and your child. So I have taught my kids to only come to me to talk about this, as other kids – and especially adults – will make fun of them. When they see a spirit, I tell my children to say to it in a loud and firm voice, "In the name of Jesus, go away!" This is a sure means to make these things disappear. I remind my kids of the superhero analogy – that this is one of the special powers they can call on. No, they're not crazy; just deal with the situation and get on with what you were doing.

Ten years ago, we were living in a city on a property that backed onto a wealthy, gated community. One night around mid-evening, I was hanging out washing under cover on our balcony when I suddenly heard the unnerving noise of tyres screeching on the palm tree-lined main road that runs through that well-heeled housing estate behind us. CRASH! The persistent drone of a broken car horn followed the terrible noise of crunching metal, and smoke billowed into the air above the trees not too far from us. Someone had been driving recklessly on that road, lost control of their car and crashed into one of the palm trees. I was about to go inside and call emergency services when I noticed the lights of other vehicles arriving and the drivers stopping to offer assistance. The young man at the wheel, who had just recently become a father, was pronounced dead at the scene.

Two months later, I was chatting with my daughter when we both heard a man talking to my two-year-old son, who was playing with his toy cars outside on the balcony. My daughter and I instantly stopped talking, momentarily glanced at each other with vexation and then scrambled outside, but no one was there. The balcony gate was shut, and it was difficult for anyone to access the area where my son was playing. My son looked up at me and smiled as I asked him if he was talking to a man. To my astonishment, he said he *was* talking to a man, and he even told me the man's name. Robert said he was on the balcony stairs asking my son's name and if he liked living next to a park with kangaroos.

When I asked my son where the man had gone (because we'd stepped out on the balcony so quickly that there was no time for anyone to leave without us seeing them), he said, "He disappeared, mummy." I sensed danger, so I bustled my kids inside the house and locked the doors. I then went on the Internet and Googled the name of the car crash victim. Sure enough, it was the same name! This man, who had passed away two months prior, had a conversation with my child.

The moral of the story is that your ASD child will likely be able to see the spiritual realm. It would be best not to ridicule them but rather to give them a sense of power over what to do in these situations. By supporting your child through strange and unusual incidents, you can reinforce relationships and form tight emotional bonds with them.

CHAPTER 19
WHAT I HAVE LEARNT ON THIS INCREDIBLE JOURNEY

My mother is notably absent from the book because she is a private person and doesn't want to be discussed. After reaching out to her and sharing my thoughts, I have been given her permission for this personal reflection. I have had an epiphany regarding my mother and myself when I was Ruby's age. I was Ruby, and my mother was me when I was 20 years old and experienced similar mental health issues. An abusive relationship at 15 and hormonal problems caused me to lose my way.

My mother was a tower of strength and took me to see specialists, stayed up on suicide watch and provided unconditional love and support during this difficult time. I want to express my profound gratitude to my mother for not giving up on me. Your actions have shaped my life and inspired me to be a tower of strength for my children, just as you were for me.

There are two life lessons I learnt from my own mum:

1. Vitamin supplements are so important, as being run down can make mental health issues worse.
2. Avoid having a victim mentality. She taught me that bad things happen to everyone, and the key is to keep going and finish the race. She showed me that help is always there when you stumble, ready to pick you back up and help you persevere to the finish line.

My parents have been married for many years, and my mother's resilience has been a constant inspiration. My mother has stood by my father through numerous health crises. I often reflect on her life experience in her early 20s when her fiancé came close to death, resulting in the amputation of his leg. She spent countless hours by his side during his rehabilitation, learning to walk again with a prosthetic limb. Her dedication, love, and strength left a lasting impression on me during this time. Working at a chemist and catching public transport in winter to spend many months with him after work was a labour of love. I also experienced a similar life-death situation with my husband concerning his brain tumour. History did repeat itself for this mother and daughter. I am grateful that my mum was a positive example of how to handle a life crisis.

When I was expecting our children, I was unaware of potential health issues such as Autism Spectrum Disorder or Dissociative Identity Disorder. I was too busy nesting and preparing to welcome God's new creations into the world. The day our children enter the world is forever etched in mothers' memories.

Our daughter had the roar of a lion when she was born, but my husband and I are sure she smiled at us when we said "Hello" after the surgeons popped her up over the screen that was blocking our view of the Caesarian mess. Our son had a piercing cry but settled down quickly and wore an austere expression as he cuddled into my chest, earning himself the nickname Mister Serious. Medical issues arose as they aged: some peculiarities in their behaviour.

Our daughter 'blew raspberries' for prolonged periods as she rocked back and forth in her rocker, bellowing to the point where we wondered if she was on the brink of hyperventilating. On all fours, she head-butted her cot cyclically and hummed at length to tire herself out and fall asleep at bedtime. Once she was walking confidently, our daughter began flapping her arms and 'bouncing' – jumping on the spot excitedly. When she began having the most monumental mood swings and tantrums, her doctor told me, "Girls don't have Autism." That proved to be an astonishingly ignorant statement from a doctor, someone I trusted and who should have known better.

Our son seemed more level-headed and calm as a baby, although he had his moments as a toddler: an obsession with manholes manifested to the point where we wondered if something was amiss. Have you heard of the car-travelling game 'punch-bug' that families played in the '70s to pass the time on car trips, spotting Volkswagen Beetles and tallying the sightings? Our boy similarly busied himself, excitedly spotting manholes from the backseat of our car as we travelled around.

High Functioning Autism (ASD) and Dissociative Identity Disorder (DID) can be seen as a blessing. For me, DID is like spontaneous time-travelling, allowing me to enjoy our daughter as a little girl again. Realistically, DID presents considerable difficulties, some of which are not funny in the least. Believe it or not, ASD typically brings the blessings of special gifts to these exceptional and unique children. There are many famous and successful ASD people, including exceedingly wealthy entrepreneurs and entertainers, who are household names known the world over. Even the most cursory Google search will produce endless lists of scientists, artists, actors, musicians and business people who are 'on the Spectrum.'

On quite a few occasions when our daughter was away from home on an outing, her alter-child phoned me, distressed and agonising over her disorientation, asking, "Where am I?" and "When are you coming to pick me up?" While Ruby was staying at a specialised retreat for 'at risk' teens, Genevieve often called, crying for me to go to her and bring her home. I have also had many deep and meaningful discussions with Edmund about his existential predicament, including his body dysmorphia.

Some of these conversations have been soul-crushing for me as their mother because I adore my alter children and think of them as my own. When Ruby was diagnosed with DID, I told my tribe – my closest friends – that hubby always wanted more kids. Well, he got his wish! Many children packed into one body is budget-friendly, saving room in our house. Genevieve and Edmund are forever my alter babies. They will never age, even as they know their body is growing up, resulting in a disorientation that provokes some awkward questioning about their birthdays and their age. And yet, they will remain the same – unchanging, perfect and unique – living in that fantastic Victorian mansion inside Ruby's mind … and visiting us less often.

Ruby has excruciating physical ailments associated with her DID, such as body aches and pains, dizziness, and feeling emotionally and physically exhausted. She also has frightening memory gaps, no sense of self, flashbacks, self-destructive behaviour and depersonalisation. Our daughter is suffering, and I wish I had a magic wand to take away all the pain and tears over the years. I have learnt from my father to use humour to handle difficult situations. I get out of bed every day, unsure of what awaits me, but my sense of humour has helped me parent my superheroes.

I acknowledge that there are many health concerns, stresses, financial hardships, and moments of extreme frustration: the feeling that your child will never achieve age-appropriate milestones. But to keep us motivated and hopeful, God will produce fleeting miracles. These surprises encourage our children to achieve something for themselves. When that happens, we parents of ASD children are elated; there's no feeling quite like it. We are instantly overjoyed and motivated to confidently step out in faith in this world, trusting that through Jesus' providence, protection and provision, we can tell our children that everything is fine and they have a bright future ahead of them.

I have been deeply blessed not to have to travel this journey alone. With company, the joys are doubled, and the sorrows are halved. Statistically speaking, the majority of parents of special needs children end up separating due to the stress and hardship that raising such children places on their marriage. My husband isn't perfect, but he has a big heart and has been tenacious and resilient through all these turbulent years.

An American pastor visiting our church said, "God chose you and your husband to be parents of these amazing kids because He knew that both of you together could handle it." That message resonates with me, especially in the tough times, and I want you to remember that, too. It can be disheartening at times when your children are misbehaving, or frustration can set in at not finding the appropriate healthcare workers to attend to your children's developmental needs. Please remember this: God isn't finished with you yet. Your parental journey is like a tapestry. You can only see the mess of coloured thread at the back of the artwork. However, God sees the front in all its glory: a perfect and beautiful design, colourful and bright, which is your accomplishment as a parent of special needs kids, creating a bright future for your children.

Another big lesson is that friends and family members will likely disappoint you. They don't understand your child's medical diagnosis, and due to this lack of understanding, they will criticise your parenting. That hurts, and our specialists advised us to cut a few particularly hurtful individuals out of our children's lives. There was a lot of negativity and harsh words, criticising us behind our backs even though we did everything the specialists recommended during trying circumstances. It broke our hearts to cut people out of our lives, but it was necessary, and we are doing much better for having done so. Unfortunately, the closest people in your life can be the most damaging, and that's heartbreaking. Still, you can create a new, supportive family by contacting other families with special needs kids.

Your kids should meet other children with similar medical diagnoses so they know they are not alone. Like-minded friends going through similar challenges in life can support each other during childhood trials and rejection from kids in their schools. The reassurance of a network of supportive friends builds resilience in autistic children, who are remarkably responsive to positive reinforcement. You might even see your child smile for the first time in years. Once again, I reaffirm my admiration for single parents of special needs children. I need help doing the groundwork, with my partner providing a stable platform from which I can concentrate on mothering our children and assembling the ASD and DID jigsaw puzzle pieces.

Be prepared for rejection from Christians at churches as well. Similarly to family and friends, this is often because they don't understand disabilities and react with self-righteous indignation but, in doing so, reflect a lousy witness. I have had bad experiences at churches that believed our autistic children needed to be exorcised of demons! They appear to be unaware of the severe mental damage they can do to unique, special needs children when accusations of demonic possession are not only implied but acted upon. If it happens to your family, I advise you to leave that church immediately and not look back. Find a church that is kind and supportive towards your child or children.

In all honesty, non-Christians have shown more kindness towards my children and acceptance of their health issues than Christians have. We say *Don't let Christians get in the way of*

Jesus, though, and I should note that older Christians in their senior years have shown much greater compassion towards my kids than middle-aged and younger Christians, suggesting there's a generational or maturity issue here.

Along the same lines, don't be too trusting and open up to people in your local church unless you know these individuals won't betray your confidence. It's surprising how people who say they are your friends will turn on you and spread gossip through the church about you or your children, words that you shared in confidence. Finding people you can trust can be a painful process. It is God's job to change those who hurt you, not yours, and until that positive spiritual change occurs, give these people a wide berth and hold your tongue for those who prove themselves trustworthy.

Moving two steps forward and one step backward is normal. You will have high days when your child is doing well emotionally and achieving goals. Still, then a setback can happen, often triggered by a stray sight, word, sound or thought that fires off an anxiety-inducing memory, and the horror comes crashing back. Just hang in there, apply tender loving care, and you will see your child's health improve again. Setbacks help us appreciate our children's achievements – their emotional growth – all the more. Stand firm, pray and let God do the rest.

Every family with special needs children is unique and dances to a different tune. You need to investigate what works as you organise activities and apply parenting strategies over time. Only a few of the ideas I have presented here are likely to work for everyone. Many will likely help, but there are plenty of different strategies you can discover and try or invent for yourself. Finding an effective developmental strategy will take time. Think of parenting your child as being like a giant jigsaw puzzle. Just keep working to slot the right pieces in, one piece at a time, and if you reflect on when you started the therapy journey, you will see that your child has made significant progress over time.

Be prepared to act. If you see another mum having a rough time in public with their child having sensory overload issues, step forward and offer assistance. I have read many social media posts from mums of autistic children struggling at the supermarket who are treated terribly and ridiculed by other mums for their child's behaviour. Such ignorance and arrogance disgust me, and believe it or not, whoever does this is on God's candid camera and will be shamed for mistreating a parent who is struggling like this.

Similarly, don't take part in rumour mills. Everyone gossips, especially women; it's in our DNA. However, a Chinese whisper about a family with special needs kids can create all sorts of trouble as being accepted is already challenging for them without gossip further undermining their credibility.

My husband calls me "Mrs Kravitz," alluding to the spying, busy-body neighbour in the *Bewitched* TV sitcom because I know much of what is happening in our neighbourhood. I am an avid gardener, and while working in our garden, I pay attention to what is happening around me. Am I proud of being a snoopy, Mrs. Kravitz? No! But I don't get on the phone and spread dirt about my neighbours or anyone. That's the difference!

The Chinese whisper cyclone has happened to me on numerous occasions. Instead of checking facts, it grows into a mountain of lies that people you trust end up believing. They suddenly distance themselves from you, stop talking to you, and certainly avoid approaching you about what has been said about your family to sort the truth from the lies! This kind of behaviour is damaging and hurtful, and I still get upset that some people will deliberately sabotage your reputation to feel empowered.

Treasure your children's small achievements as they will become considerable milestones in retrospect. I have been on this remarkable journey for nearly ten years, and I am proud of my two kids. So proud! I have seen both of them experience pain, humiliation, bullying, physical and psychological bruising, and rumours and lies spread about them.

Our Wednesday and Pugsley Addams are the most precious gifts God has given me! Our daughter's quick-witted, dry humour and snarky remarks, and my son's hilarious, cooky gags that have me in stitches are some qualities I love about them. Because of the adversity she has dealt with, our daughter is kind and patient around other people with disabilities, and so she is training in support work for special needs people. I have often told her that the way to heal is to pay it forward: the fact that she has had all these life experiences and has learnt from them makes her uniquely equipped to help others in this area. Now, that is a blessing!

Our son readily apologises after misbehaving. He is thoughtful and sweet. Robert often says things that may not be politically correct but are usually insightful, paradoxical, quirky, and funny. When he walks into a room, he instantly brightens everyone's day. Humouring through painful life lessons and growing experiences is a gift. A good sense of humour is the secret to facing life's trials and tribulations.

CHAPTER 20
CRAZY MOTHER'S GUIDE TO RAISING EXCEPTIONAL CHILDREN – THE 12 PRINCIPLES

This chapter combines my parenting ideas into simple rules or guidelines to help you make the most of my memoir as 'warden' of our 'asylum.' You may want to write down the key points and display them on your fridge door to be regularly reminded of them. I know all mums are busy, so this list will help you focus on achieving your life-improvement goals for your ASD child or children.

1. **Rome wasn't built in a day.** Finding the proper treatment, therapy, and support workers that fit your jigsaw puzzle takes much time and effort, trial and error. It can take years of trials and emotional pain before your child starts to move forward and achieve significant life achievements. There will be small victories along the way to keep you both motivated and not give up on reaching your ultimate goals.

2. **God has deliberately chosen you to parent your kids because He knows you can handle it.** The Divine Creator of the Universe picked you because He knew you would do a fantastic job. Hold onto this thought during rough days. It was like a light bulb switched on inside my head when an American minister said this to me. So I cling to this thought like a life preserver when I'm suddenly thrown overboard, out of my safe and familiar world and into murky, treacherous waters.

3. **Be prepared to be unfairly judged and criticised.** Your parenting skills will be closely scrutinised by close family members and friends who don't understand special needs children or the strange solutions and techniques you come up with. You may have to cut family members or friends out of your life if they attempt to undermine your efforts or spread gossip about you. This is because such harmful interference will adversely impact your family unit. These individuals don't understand your unique situation, and the fallout from their meddling can cause potentially life-threatening problems for your children. If your medical professionals suggest removing

certain people from your life for your children's sake, please follow their advice.

4. **Keep the faith and pray for spiritual guidance.** This includes asking others in your church to pray for your family. Having a godly Christian mentor you can turn to with concerns about your family is a great help, especially in times of trouble. Our family has been blessed to have Chris and Sandy J., who have been in our lives for over 27 years. Without their support and wisdom, our family would have struggled much more to survive the immense pressure we had to endure. These two lovebirds exemplify how a minister and his better half should act and effectively respond to their flock's life struggles.

5. **Be kind to yourself.** Life is about learning from our mistakes and moving forward. Be kind to other parents of special needs children, too, and do not gossip or criticise their parenting skills. There is no instruction book for exceptional kids, but I can tell you I wish there were. It is all about trial and error. In the past, I have criticised other special needs parents, and I am ashamed

that I have done this, but I have learnt from being on the receiving end that it's a nasty, hurtful thing to do.

6. **Make sure you don't neglect your spouse or partner.** It could be a date night or simply a walk together alone. Our home is like Central Station, with support workers and other medical professionals coming and going. Finding 'together time' for my husband and I has become quite challenging as our lives are hectic. We used to go on short getaways for a couple of days once a year. Unfortunately, that has been put on hold due to our son's severe separation anxiety issues. But this will pass, and in the meantime, we often sneak little kisses and cuddles through the day and take advantage of little breaks from parenting to reconnect during the week when a therapist or tutor is in session with our kids or a support worker takes them out for the day.

7. **Knowledge and wisdom are key.** It might seem a bit obvious, but it is crucial to research, read, learn and understand as much as you can about your child's disability. There's plenty of information on the Internet and in libraries; ask your local librarian; they'll be happy to help. There are fantastic, free,

online short courses in disability care, especially in parenting kids on the Spectrum. I highly recommend doing a course like this, as it helped me to see the world from my child's perspective when I was pretty confused just after my children's diagnoses.

8. **Trial and error.** Some things work; others don't. When they don't, try something else. Keep thinking outside the box and find the missing puzzle pieces. Keep a written account, like a journal, of what works and what doesn't. This will help in the future when a medical specialist asks you what medications, treatments or therapies your child has tried and how they responded.

9. **Don't adopt a victim mentality.** As a parent, you must adopt a warrior mentality to fight for your children, who count on you to help them. Don't give up trying new forms of therapy. Persevere, stay positive, do the work, and pray that God will reveal the answers you need to help your children.

10. **Network with other parents.** Form relationships with other parents who are in similar circumstances to your own. Cultivate

both online and in-person friendships to ensure you have companions who understand your challenges. You can provide mutual comfort and support while exchanging treatment ideas and parenting strategies by having someone to confide in, whether you need to talk, cry, or vent.

11. **A sense of humour.** I always wanted to marry someone with a good sense of humour, and luckily, I have that in my husband. My dad showed me how a sense of humour helped him through the worst, most painful days of being an amputee. So our home has a lot of laughter, mainly because our son has the most amazing, funny way with words; he is always quick with witty one-liners. But my husband also has a knack for dropping the most unexpected and inventive hilarity bombs. I have often left the room because I have been physically hurt from laughing too much. My husband's humour is usually too dry for most to notice, so I'm thrilled I can catch his finesse gags when no one else gets them. It's a form of deeper understanding and intimacy in our relationship. Our love language is laughter, and I cherish it daily.

12. **Frequently review the past to know where you're heading in the future.** This is about reflection. Keep notes of your child's progress over the years so you can look back and see how far you have come. This is a great incentive to inspire you during days of hardship. Should you need more help, such notes or journals will help inform health professionals.

CHAPTER 21
WHAT DOES YOUR FUTURE HOLD?

I want to empower mothers of special needs children by creating a worldwide network of support groups. You can create communal bonds with like-minded parents in similar circumstances by reaching out on my social media Facebook page. Information regarding how to become involved is in the back of this book.

Your future is in God's hands. But you also have the power to take control of your own life. This book is a labour of love for me. Years ago, when I started this journey with our kids, I felt helpless and alone. I would try to befriend women in the rural community we moved to, but once they saw how crazy my family life was, they didn't want a bar of me or my children. My kids were never mean or hurtful to other kids – in fact, they were the opposite – they couldn't have been more accommodating. They were polite and sweet, letting the visiting children play with their toys and do whatever they wanted. But the rumour mill at the local church was in full swing, so it didn't matter what I would say to the ladies; I still had two heads, and my kids still had a contagious disease such that no one wanted to know us.

The funny thing is the mothers judging me had kids who were displaying atrocious behaviour, and these parents were in ministry leadership. But I was blessed to find one fantastic friend in my local community named Tess, the mother of a special needs child, who listened to me and guided me when I wanted to download. She never gave up on me, and even though she relocated to a new area, I think of her fondly for her kindness. Those women at church could learn something about the love of Christ and extend the hand of friendship to strangers from this outstanding individual who is also a church-goer.

Have Faith: your children will achieve their growth milestones; it just takes time and patience. Remember the tapestry analogy? We only see the tangle of coloured thread at the back, but God sees the finished work. I have also 'grown up' a lot since becoming a parent of special needs children and have become more patient and kind to others, especially those who have physical or mental health issues. I have always danced to a different tune and loved being around people considered social outcasts through no fault of their own. My amputee father showed me that you can achieve anything if you persevere.

My husband showed me that you can dress differently and still be Christian because God looks at our hearts rather than our fashion sense. I might not have been saved without hubby coming into my life and teaching me this valuable lesson. Experimenting with clothes and hair is a rather superficial pursuit on the face of it, but it can connect you to a subcultural tribe. For special needs kids, donning a 'superhero' costume or disguise can be just the ticket to empowering them to step outside the door and face their phobias. Stepping out into the big wide world is a crucial step in a special needs child's development, especially if they have or had an agoraphobia-like dread of leaving the comfort of their own homes, perhaps as a reaction to some past abuse.

Fuelled by exposure to her father's '70s and '80s alternative music collection, our daughter needed a visual disguise to make her more comfortable being out in public. So, I encouraged her to experiment with hair colours and alternative fashion from about her mid-teens. Being homeschooled, she could freely experiment with her appearance. From my experience, I already knew I could socialise with others better when dressed in Goth clothing. I wasn't surprised that my daughter felt empowered by changing her appearance and readily ventured into the world to show off her metamorphosis.

At the time of writing, our daughter is nearly 20 and has toned down her hair colours, which I knew would happen as she became more confident within herself. Her dress sense is exquisite, as she carefully crafts her unique ensembles, combining pieces found in opportunity (thrift) shops with new and second-hand items of clothing bought online. She often comes home excited, telling me how strangers complimented her on her look. Her eyes grow wide with glee, and my heart melts with happiness for her. She is finally seeing what I have known all along: that she is beautiful inside and out, and the years of being tormented by other children were coming from their envy; they resented how pretty and smart she was. My daughter has had all the colours of the rainbow rinsed through her naturally beautiful, strawberry-blonde locks. She has facial piercings, which I'm not crazy about, but I knew she wanted them to mark her triumph of survival.

So what do you do if your child has just been diagnosed with autism and you're new to parenting special needs kids? It would be best to get advice from those who have been in your situation. Reach out and network with other women who have been on this roller coaster ride for a long time. Many mums are willing to help you, but you must be brave enough to ask for advice first.

Build a schedule and implement daily routines so that there is some semblance of order in the child's life. Remember to include plenty of free and fun time in the schedule so their lives don't feel too regimented. Get professional help as soon as possible, including beginning your search for suitable support workers. Please do your due diligence in researching and becoming informed about your child's condition and health needs, then closely monitor and record their health care.

The most important thing to remember is that although your life may suddenly feel doubly chaotic with all the medical appointments, time management issues, crazy children's behaviour, and your exhaustion and disorientation like you've been thrown overboard from a ship ... things will improve. Stay close to Jesus through prayer, read your Bible, and consult with genuine, humble, loving, trustworthy, God-fearing Christians who will support and minister to you and your family. I have been doing this for a long time, and our precious daughter is making astonishing progress. She has received art awards, pursued a higher education qualification and learned to drive. These achievements follow her learning to regulate her emotions to attend rock concerts, even standing in the front row for entire shows. Years ago, she wouldn't even step out of our home, let alone attend a concert with thousands of people.

Recently, my son has been diagnosed with Ehler-Danlos syndrome, which describes unstable joints that are prone to dislocation. This is new for me, so I am currently researching treatments and therapy options for my son, and I have employed the services of a physiotherapist with expertise in this area to help him. She knows which targeted exercises can help strengthen his joints. Our son, who is only 12 years of age, has already gone through puberty but handled the distress of his body changes with surprising resilience. Although he does have the occasional fit of anxiety. God has created an amazing young man who is also artistic, funny, and gifted. He lights up any room with his beaming smile and quick-witted humour. I am so proud of my children and also those I have adopted: friends of my kids who have similar issues and who I have taken under my wing as some of them are also 'at risk.'

My husband has also grown in leaps and bounds and has developed considerable patience for the daily madness that our home life is subjected to. He's not perfect, but his love of Jesus and his family and his quest for self-improvement are inspiring. We recently received compliments on how warm, inviting, and peaceful our house is. We put that down to our faith and thank God that our love of Jesus permeates our home to the point that visitors notice the difference. I keep telling my kids that Jesus was the first alternative person in the entire world, as he would rather spend time with lost souls who needed guidance than with religious hypocrites.

As for me, God and my children have made me a better person. I was selfish and self-absorbed until my kids came into my life and taught me unconditional love, patience and acceptance of the unique and creative people in this world. It doesn't take much to say a kind word to a mother whose child is having a sensory meltdown at the local supermarket. Don't stand there and judge; offer to help. Ask the frazzled mother if there is anything you can do for her. This poor woman may have other kids who need her attention as well.

Creative people must do something that inspires their souls in their free time. I love painting landscapes but haven't found the time. I enjoy creative writing, but until recently, I have had to put everything on hold to concentrate on my children's mental and physical well-being. Now that I am writing again, I feel my God-given spirit come alive as I download my thoughts and feelings on parenting entertainingly. Try allocating 15—20 minutes daily to your favourite artistic pursuits, whether gardening, writing, music, pottery or painting. By doing this, you will slowly see a more positive attitude within you shining forth.

I have also learned that there will be days when the circus is in town, but I am the ringleader of my sideshow, and I can be a better mother. I can stop cursing when something goes wrong and control my mega-momma meltdowns when I resemble a crazy Karen or a Kraken from the deep. Life is about making mistakes, learning from them, and doing better in the future.

Be kind to other mothers and start working to develop valuable connections with other special needs families. One of my favourite quotes is from the 1971 movie *Willy Wonka & the Chocolate Factory* – the adaptation of Roald Dahl's 1964 book. Towards the end of the movie, Charlie is rejected by Wonka. Yet, the boy selflessly gives his Everlasting Gobstopper back to Wonka. By doing this one simple, selfless act, Charlie effectively refuses arch-enemy Slugworth's offer of a reward for betraying Wonka by delivering that top-secret confectionery to him. Seeing Charlie's honesty, Wonka – memorably portrayed by Gene Wilder – whispers, ***"So shines a good deed in a weary world"*** (Stuart, M. 1971).

Let us be that beacon of light and initiate positive change together with other parents of children with special needs in our community. These remarkable individuals deserve our unwavering support and encouragement. Let's reach out to families whose children have recently been diagnosed with severe medical conditions. They may feel daunted or overwhelmed by the challenges of parenting in such circumstances.

While we cannot control the future or change the past, we can actively work to help our children achieve their life goals today. Let's commit to spreading kindness and positivity in this weary world through our loving words and good deeds towards one another. ***Together, we can make a difference!***

Sonia D. Hebdon

REFERENCES

Dahl, R. (2005) *Charlie & the Chocolate Factory*. New York: Puffin.

Epictetus (1997) *The Golden Sayings of Epictetus*. Project Guttenberg.

Gloom, R. (2024). *Ruby Gloom theme song*. (Online) Ruby Gloom Wiki. Available at: https://rubygloom.fandom.com/wiki/Theme_song (Accessed 22 Oct. 2024).

NIV Bible, New International Version (2007). London: Hodder & Stoughton Ltd.

Rik Mayall, *Drop Dead Fred.* May, 1991 (Film, USA) Universal Pictures, New Line Cinema, The Rank Organisation.

Rik Mayall, starring as Rick in *The Young Ones* (1982-1984), a British TV Situation Comedy written by Rik Mayall, Ben Elton, and Lise Mayer, BBC2 England.

Stuart, M. (1971) *Willy Wonka & the Chocolate Factory*. (Film, USA). Warner Bros Studio.

ABOUT THE AUTHOR

Sonia grew up in a coastal town in North Queensland, Australia, and moved to Sydney in the early '90s to attend university. She earned a degree in Liberal Studies, with majors in Literary Theory and Communications, from the University of Western Sydney. While studying at UWS, she met her partner in crime and created a unique family together. She worked in radio, public relations, and education before focusing on her family.

Sonia is passionate about her faith and the acceptance of individuals with disabilities. Her father, an amputee, greatly influenced her perspective, so she has always danced to her own tune, embracing unique individuals as 'superheroes'.

OTHER TITLES BY SONIA D. HEBDON

Sonia has developed a Christian Early Reader Series designed especially for Primary School-aged children on the Autism Spectrum, aged 6—8. The ***I Am Perfect The Way I Am*** series focuses on boosting children's confidence once they have been diagnosed and know they are different.

Vlad McCoy, A Unique Vampire Boy

Vlad McCoy is no ordinary vampire boy. He is unique because he can walk in sunlight, eat human food, and prefers to smile instead of frown. His best friend is human, which worries his vampire parents. Why is their son so different?

Ruby Ray Is Only A Dream Away!

Ruby Ray has a job to do.
God has gifted her,
To deliver sweet dreams to you!
Now, she doesn't have plenty of time.
But she will do her best to deliver,
Before the grandfather clock's
Midnight chime.

I Am A SuperHero

These children all have super
powers like you! They have Autism
Spectrum Disorder (or ASD).
This makes them Superheroes.
Do you want to know why?
Read the book and find out.

Remember, all kids with disabilities
Are Superheroes. You just need to find
Out what superpower you have.

SONIA D. HEBDON: SOCIAL MEDIA

Website:

thecrazymothersguidetoparentingexceptionalchildren.org

Facebook:

https://www.facebook.com/profile.php?id=61569399597133

The Crazy Mother's Guide To Parenting Exceptional Children **Private Support Group:**

https://www.facebook.com/groups/180350565712 4738/

Email:

soniadhebdon@gmail.com

BEAUTIFUL DESERT: Alternative Christian Music Ministry, '80s Style!

https://www.youtube.com/@beautifuldesert7757

PHILIPPIANS 2:4

"Don't look out only for your own interests, but take an interest in others, too."

www.ingramcontent.com/pod-product-compliance
Lightning Source LLC
Chambersburg PA
CBHW080553090426
42735CB00016B/3221